A STUDY OF THE BOOK OF MATTHEW

A Better Way

> HOW JESUS' LIFE GUIDES US TO PEACE IN A WORLD THAT STEALS OUR SANITY

Written by: Kayla Ferris

© 2022 by Proverbs 31 Ministries

All Scripture quotations are English Standard Version (ESV) unless otherwise noted.

WE MUST EXCHANGE *whispers* WITH GOD BEFORE *shouts* WITH THE WORLD.

LYSA TERKEURST

PAIR YOUR STUDY GUIDE WITH THE FIRST 5 MOBILE APP!

This study guide is designed to accompany your study of Scripture in the First 5 mobile app.

You can use it as a standalone study, or as an accompanying guide to the daily content within First 5.

First 5 is a free mobile app developed by Proverbs 31 Ministries to transform your daily time with God.

Go to the app store on your smartphone, download the First 5 app and create a free account!

WWW.FIRST5.ORG

MATTHEW 11:29

"Take my *yoke* upon you, and *learn* from me, for I am *gentle* and *lowly* in heart, and you will find *rest* for your *souls.*"

WELCOME TO Matthew

A while back, my family started having car problems. It finally reached the point where the car had to be taken to a mechanic. They were able to fix the problem, and the car drove like a dream ... until two days later when the brake pads started squealing every time we stopped. I thought to myself, *Seriously?! This car is driving me crazy!*

Not only when it comes to my car but when it comes to everyday life, it seems like every time I turn around there is a new problem, new conflict, new "bad news." The list of things to stress and lose sleep over is long. And as I cycle through feelings of worry, anxiety and sometimes even panic, there is this voice in the back of my head that keeps saying, *There has to be a better way to live!*

Friends, **there is.** There is a better way! This world, with its problems and worries and chaos, isn't going to change. But that doesn't mean we have to let it steal our sanity. It is possible to find peace in the middle of it all! That peace, **that better way, is found in Jesus.**

Over the next eight weeks, we are going to study the life of Jesus as recorded in the book of Matthew. The world outside of Jesus' life was as chaotic as it gets. Harsh empires, murderous rulers, suffering and hurting people. The world around Jesus did not have peace. In fact, Jesus Himself said, *"Do not think that I have come to bring peace to the earth"* (Matthew 10:34a). Jesus acknowledged that this world is a mess. Yet even though there is not peace on earth, there is peace in Jesus. His peace was completely solid and unbreakable, even to the point of death.

Jesus did not just live out peace, but He also shared words of wisdom to help guide us toward a life of peace as well. In fact, 60% of Matthew contains teachings and guidance that Jesus personally spoke while on earth.[1] Jesus' words will be a lamp for our feet and a light for our path (Psalm 119:105) as we journey toward peace.

So friends, are you tired of the chaos? Are you ready for a better way? Jesus' path toward peace will not necessarily calm the chaos around you, but as many of us have already experienced, it will absolutely calm the chaos inside. And as His peace fills your heart and mind, maybe you will find that you can breathe a little deeper, sleep a little sounder and feel a little more sane. Welcome to the book of Matthew.

WHY IS THIS WORLD SO *Chaotic?*

Within this study guide, you will find a special section each weekend that will take us along a path toward peace. By studying Jesus' life within the book of Matthew, we are going to see a better way to live. A life with King Jesus can provide a peace *"which surpasses all understanding"* (Philippians 4:7).

If we take a look at the world around us, peace seems to be running short. With so little peace, it is no wonder we can start to feel like the world is stealing our sanity. But why is that exactly? We can say it's from the mounting pressures of money, jobs, family and time. It might be wars, terrorists, diseases, pandemics and death. Perhaps it's the increasing pace of life; the internet; "smart" devices; or media, both social and news. And while these all play a part in the chaos our world is experiencing, there seems to be another interesting force at play in our world today.

According to the Pew Research Center, the number of people in the U.S. who identify as "Christian" has dropped significantly between 2007 and 2021. In 2007, 78% of people polled said they were Christian. In 2021, that number dropped to 63%. That is a 15% loss! And where are most of these people going? According to the study, people who identify as being "no religion" went from 16% in 2007 to a startling 29% in 2021.[1] If these patterns continue, there could soon come a time when Christianity is no longer the majority religion in this part of the world. Western culture confirms this trend as it becomes increasingly antagonistic toward Christianity. So what does this have to do with peace?

Those who push away from Christianity (and more specifically, King Jesus), will find themselves further and further away from true peace. Chaos will only grow. Jesus predicted this Himself when He said, *"Behold, I am sending you out as sheep in the midst of wolves"* (Matthew 10:16). This world is going to be wild and savage because the world is missing the point of it all. See, the world wants a perfect kingdom but without **the King**. However, the only perfect Kingdom is Jesus'. There is no true civility, no true peace, without Jesus.

So the world outside will rage and threaten, my friends. That isn't going to stop. But **peace is possible**. Jesus said to those who follow Him, *"the one who endures to the end will be saved"* (Matthew 10:22b). Jesus' life shows us that we can leave behind the ways of the world and find peace in walking with Him.

ALL ABOUT THE *Author*

It might surprise you to learn that none of the four Gospel accounts in the New Testament has the author's name recorded as such. This means, technically, they are all anonymous. However, we do have reliable historical documents that have helped scholars make an educated guess at who these authors were. In documents written by church leaders as early as the second century, the particular Gospel account we are studying is said to have been written by a man named Matthew, a former tax collector who became one of Jesus' 12 disciples.

We learn a little of Matthew's story through the other Gospel accounts. He was also called Levi the son of Alphaeus. (Mark 2:14) It was not unusual during this time period to have more than one name. It could also be that Levi was given a new name when he decided to follow Christ. The name Matthew means "the gift of God."

The story of Matthew's call to follow Jesus is recorded in Matthew 9:9-17. From here, we learn Matthew was a tax collector. Tax collectors were among the most hated groups of people in Judea. Jewish tax collectors were considered traitors because they worked alongside the Romans. Men like Matthew were called thieves for taking money from their fellow Jews. The more taxes the collectors took, the more money they made. Therefore, many tax collectors were made wealthy by taking heavy taxes, which left the people with almost nothing. Tax collectors were also seen as ceremonially unclean because of their frequent contact with gentiles. Rejected and despised, tax collectors were associated with the likes of prostitutes and other "notorious" sinners.

Yet what the world rejected, Jesus called His own. Matthew's calling was divine. He had a unique perspective. Being Jewish, he would have been familiar with the Old Testament laws and prophecies. Being a tax collector, Matthew would have been trained in scribal techniques. In other words, he could write. Alexander Whyte of Edinburgh once said that when Matthew left his job to follow Christ, he brought his pen with him.[1] And we are so grateful he did!

There is a beautiful little detail in the story of Matthew's calling. Matthew left his tax booth and made Jesus a great feast in his house. (Luke 5:29) The Pharisees were upset and asked, *"Why does your teacher eat with tax collectors and sinners?"* (Matthew 9:11). Jesus said He did not come for the well or the righteous but for the sick and the sinners. (Matthew 9:13) Friends, that meant tax collectors and prostitutes, but it also meant Pharisees and religious leaders. Simply put, Jesus had not come to call the righteous because there were none righteous.

Jesus had come for sinners in need of a Savior. That means all of us. We can marvel at how Jesus chose someone like Matthew, but we also marvel at how Jesus came for people like us. Oh, what a Savior He is!

THE *Four* GOSPELS

The first four books of the New Testament are called the Gospels. The word "gospel" is translated from the Greek word *euangelion,* which means "good news." Each of these four Gospel accounts offers a unique perspective on the life of Jesus. It is like four different artists, in this case all directed by the Holy Spirit, each trying to capture the same scene. While the subject is the same, their viewpoints are different. Let's take a brief overview of each Gospel account to see what makes it unique.

Matthew

WRITTEN BY
Matthew, a former tax collector and one of the 12 disciples of Jesus.

AUDIENCE
Mostly Jewish readers.

TIME IT WAS WRITTEN
A.D. late 50s-early 60s.

MAIN IDEA
Jesus is the King, the long-awaited Messiah.

Mark

WRITTEN BY
John Mark, a missionary with Paul and also a close companion to the Apostle Peter (one of the 12 disciples of Jesus). It is thought that Peter passed on stories of Jesus to John Mark.

AUDIENCE
Written from Rome, and therefore to Roman readers, but also the Church at large.

TIME IT WAS WRITTEN
A.D. mid-to-late 50s. It is thought to be the first Gospel account recorded. Some suggest that Matthew relied heavily on Mark's account.

MAIN IDEA
Jesus is a servant leader, and He calls His followers to discipleship.

WRITTEN BY
Luke, a physician who traveled with Paul. Luke is the only Gospel account recorded by a gentile.

AUDIENCE
Gentile Christians.

TIME IT WAS WRITTEN
A.D. early 60s.

MAIN IDEA
Jesus is the Savior of sinners, both Jews and gentiles alike.

WRITTEN BY
John, the son of Zebedee, one of the 12 disciples of Jesus.

AUDIENCE
Universal, written to both Jews and gentiles in the Church at large.

TIME IT WAS WRITTEN
Sometime between A.D. 70 and 100.

MAIN IDEA
Saving faith is found in knowing Jesus is the resurrected Son of God.

THE STRUCTURE OF *Matthew*

It is important when studying the book of Matthew that we are aware of its structure. Matthew was not written in chronological order. This is why the events in Matthew don't all sync with the timeline of events in the other Gospels. Instead, Matthew wrote his Gospel in topical order; he chose stories and teachings that helped illuminate his main ideas.

Within the book of Matthew, we will find five groupings or topics. Each grouping begins with narrative (story) and then moves into a section of teachings from Jesus. Each section then ends with a transition statement along the lines of "When Jesus had finished [these sayings]..." See the "5 Groupings Within Matthew" chart on the following page to find a breakdown of each group.

Matthew records over 20 miracles performed by Jesus. However, 60% of the book is focused on the teachings of Jesus. These words of Jesus truly ring throughout the ages. Also within Matthew, there are many references to the Old Testament. Matthew's goal was to show his Jewish brothers and sisters that Jesus was the King promised from the line of David, the Messiah they had been looking for their entire lives. He frequently cited Old Testament prophecies to prove just that. Because of this, Matthew makes the perfect bridge between the Old Testament and the New Testament (which is why we find Matthew listed as the first book of the New Testament instead of Mark, which is thought to be the first Gospel to have been written.)

By stepping back and seeing the overview of Matthew's structure, we are better prepared to understand the placement and significance of certain stories and teachings.

Five GROUPINGS WITHIN MATTHEW

GROUP	NARRATIVE VERSES	TEACHING VERSES	MAIN IDEA OF TEACHINGS	TRANSITION
1	Matthew 1-4	Matthew 5-7	How are we to live as citizens of the Kingdom of God?	Matthew 7:28: *"And when Jesus finished these sayings ..."*
2	Matthew 8-9:34	Matthew 9:35–10:42	How are traveling disciples to conduct themselves?	Matthew 11:1: *"When Jesus had finished instructing his twelve disciples ..."*
3	Matthew 11:2-12:50	Matthew 13:1-52	What parables did Jesus teach?	Matthew 13:53: *"And when Jesus had finished these parables ..."*
4	Matthew 13:54-17:27	Matthew 18	What warnings are there about unforgiveness and hindering someone from entering the Kingdom?	Matthew 19:1: *"Now when Jesus had finished these sayings ..."*
5	Matthew 19:2-23:39	Matthew 24-25	How will human history end?	Matthew 26:1: *"When Jesus had finished all these sayings ..."*

PATH TOWARD *Peace*

PEACE IS NOT THE ABSENCE
OF PROBLEMS.

PEACE CANNOT BE
MANUFACTURED.

PEACE WITH GOD
DOES NOT ALWAYS
MEAN PEACE WITH
OTHERS.

THERE IS NO
PEACE WITHOUT
JESUS.

PEACE COMES FROM
KNOWING THE ONE
WHO PROVIDES.

PEACE WITH
OTHERS BEGINS BY
KNOWING OUR OWN
HEARTS.

PEACE IS KEEPING
OUR EYES ON
ETERNITY WITH
JESUS.

PEACE IS POSSIBLE BECAUSE JESUS
IS ALIVE.

Major MOMENTS

Week 1

PSALM 89 - God promised a forever King from the line of David.

MATTHEW 1 - Jesus, the Messiah, was born from the line of David and yet was also divine.

MATTHEW 2 - Jesus' childhood was difficult but divinely planned.

MATTHEW 3 - John the Baptizer baptized Jesus, and the Trinity rejoiced.

MATTHEW 4 - Jesus resisted temptation and began His ministry.

Week 2

MATTHEW 5:1-12 - Jesus began His Sermon on the Mount with the Beatitudes.

MATTHEW 5:13-48 - Jesus fulfilled the law and explained that sin is a heart issue.

MATTHEW 6:1-18 - Jesus taught that motive matters.

MATTHEW 6:19-34 - Jesus taught about treasure.

MATTHEW 7 - Jesus shared the importance of discernment.

Week 3

PSALM 37 - The meek shall inherit the land.

MATTHEW 8 - Jesus demonstrated His authority.

MATTHEW 9 - Jesus had authority over sin and death because Jesus is God.

MATTHEW 10 - Jesus called His disciples and gave instructions for both then and now.

MATTHEW 11 - Jesus addressed doubt, unbelief and striving.

Week 4

MATTHEW 12:1-37 - Opposition to Jesus continued to rise.

MATTHEW 12:38-50 - Jesus said He is the greater Priest, Prophet and King.

MATTHEW 13:1-23 - Jesus said there would be varying responses to His message.

MATTHEW 13:24-43 - Jesus said true and false believers will be separated in the end.

MATTHEW 13:44-58 - Jesus taught that the Kingdom of heaven is like a great treasure.

Week 5

PSALM 69 - God will save His people from the sinking mire.
MATTHEW 14 - Jesus provided food for the crowds and safety for His disciples.
MATTHEW 15 - Jesus taught that it isn't the outside but the heart that matters.
MATTHEW 16 - Peter confessed that Jesus was the Christ, the Son of the living God.
MATTHEW 17 - Jesus demonstrated His divinity.

Week 6

MATTHEW 18 - Jesus taught humility, church discipline and forgiveness.
MATTHEW 19 - Jesus' teachings were often countercultural.
MATTHEW 20 - Jesus taught and demonstrated that the first will be last and that greatness is found in serving.
MATTHEW 21:1-22 - Jesus began His final week by boldly entering Jerusalem and the temple.
MATTHEW 21:23-46 - Jesus knew the hearts and plans of the religious leaders.

Week 7

PSALM 22 - God is present and faithful, even when His people experience great suffering.
MATTHEW 22 - Religious leaders attempted to trap Jesus with words.
MATTHEW 23 - Jesus denounced the religious leaders.
MATTHEW 24 - Jesus prophesied the end.
MATTHEW 25 - Jesus illustrated how to be ready for His return.

Week 8

MATTHEW 26:1-35 - Jesus prepared His disciples for His coming death.
MATTHEW 26:36-75 - Jesus was betrayed, arrested and taken to a Jewish hearing.
MATTHEW 27:1-31 - Jesus faced a Roman hearing and was sentenced to be crucified.
MATTHEW 27:32-66 - Jesus died and was buried in a tomb.
MATTHEW 28 - Jesus rose to life!

WE*one* EK

WEEK 1 / DAY 1

MAJOR MOMENT
God promised a forever King from the line of David.

Friends, welcome to Day 1 of our Matthew study. And yes, interestingly enough, we will not be starting in Matthew today but in Psalm, where we find what scholars call "messianic psalms." These psalms speak of the Messiah, whom we know to be Jesus Christ. By looking into Psalm 89, we are going to see a picture of Jesus that Matthew so clearly wants us to see as well.

- Psalm 89:1 says: *"… with my mouth I will make known your _____ to all generations."* What does this word mean, and what does it say about God?

- In Psalm 89:3, God said He has made a covenant with who?

- And according to Psalm 89:4, what is that covenant promise?

This is important. God promised that David's line and throne will be *"forever."* Therefore, we understand this to mean the promised Messiah will have some kind of relation to the line of David. Then something interesting is said in Psalm 89:26 …

- According to this verse, what familial term will the Messiah cry out and call God?

- Let's take a sneak peek. What do you read in Matthew 26:39?

Going on to Psalm 89:27 ...
- God says, *"And I will make him the _____,"*

- What do you learn in Colossians 1:15?

- Psalm 89:27 also says He will be what?

- What title does Paul give Jesus in 1 Timothy 6:15?

- How does Revelation 1:5 use both of these terms we find in Psalm 89:27?

The Messiah, from the line of David, would be a King. Not *just* a king but the *"highest of the kings"* (Psalm 89:27). This was God's promise. And God is faithful ... right?

- Read Psalm 89:38-39. What is the psalmist's complaint?

To the psalmist, in the current circumstance, it did not **look** or **feel** like God was keeping His promise. Have you ever been there? I have. It is a hard place to be. However, it is OK, friends, to admit this. God is big enough to handle our questions and doubts, and we can take them to Him.

- What questions do you have for God today? What might happen if you honestly and humbly bring those straight to His throne today?

Even though the psalmist couldn't see or feel it, the truth was that God did keep His covenant promise. And He is still keeping it today. We know because we can read all about it in books like Matthew. Jesus is the proof of God's faithfulness.

- Does what we see and feel always equal the truth? Why or why not?

- What are you reminded about God's faithfulness today?

WEEK 1 / DAY 2

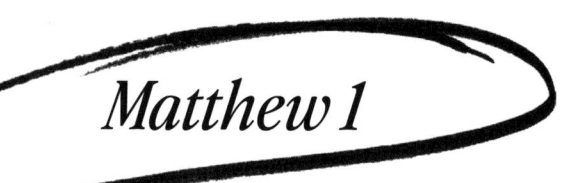

MAJOR MOMENT

Jesus, the Messiah, was born from the line of David and yet was also divine.

Yesterday we looked at God's promise to send a forever King from the line of David. Matthew started his Gospel account by proving Jesus is this King.

- What important historical names does Matthew mention in both Matthew 1:1 and Matthew 1:6?

There are several things to point out about genealogies, or family lineages, in the Bible. First, keeping records was incredibly important to ancient Jewish people. It was especially important to be able to prove one's lineage from Abraham and King David because of the messianic promises God had given. Second, genealogies were a lot like resumes. You did not include every person (for example, there are generations Matthew does not list), and you especially did not include the "bad" people. In regard to this latter rule, Matthew seems to do the opposite.

- Judah and Tamar are listed in Matthew 1:3. Read Genesis 38:13-18.
  What do we learn about these two?

- Rahab is listed in Matthew 1:5. What does Joshua 6:25 tell us about her?

- Even the beloved King David had marks on his reputation. What do you find in 2 Samuel 12:9?

- Matthew 1:7 lists Rehoboam. What does 2 Chronicles 12:14 say of him?

- Seeing this, how would you describe the family Jesus came from?

- Can anything "disqualify" you from being a part of the family of God? Why or why not?

Also countercultural to his time, Matthew listed women in Jesus' genealogy. Women were given very little recognition in many ancient cultures. And to make this genealogy even more "scandalous," most of these women were **not** Jewish! Rahab was Canaanite; Ruth was Moabite, and Bathsheba (the *"wife of Uriah"*) was married to a Hittite.

- Speaking of the promised Messiah in Genesis 12:3, God said, *"in you _____ the _____ of the _____ shall be blessed."* What does Jesus' genealogy here in Matthew remind us about His mission?*

*You might ask yourself as you write these words from Scripture: Why do we do fill-in-the-blanks in our study guides? Scripture is God-breathed, (2 Timothy 3:16) so we believe there is something special about writing out these precious words. We also choose the words to fill in very intentionally, causing us to pause, slow down and think carefully about particular words in a way we might not do just by reading over them. As you write these scriptures, we pray God will continue to bless your study.

With Jesus' physical (human) line established in Matthew 1:1-17, Matthew then wrote to show Jesus' divine line.

- According to Matthew 1:18, Mary was found to be with child from whom?

- What had God promised in Isaiah 7:14?

- Jesus was not like any other man from the line of David. He was Immanuel. According to Matthew 1:23, what does Immanuel mean?

Therefore, Jesus was human, and He was (and is) also God.

Matthew 1:25 ends by saying Joseph *"called his name Jesus."* Jesus was a common name during this time. However, Matthew wanted to emphasize that this particular Jesus was the **Christ**.

- Take a moment to highlight every time you see the word *"Christ"* in Matthew 1.

The Greek word *Christos* is from the Hebrew word מָשִׁיחַ (*ma.shi.ach*), meaning the anointed one. **The Messiah.** Jesus' birth was about so much more than anyone ever imagined …

- In what ways has God's faithfulness to you sometimes looked different than you imagined?

WEEK 1 / DAY 3

Matthew 2

MAJOR MOMENT

Jesus' childhood was difficult but divinely planned.

Following God is wonderful, but that does not mean it's easy. Today, let's look at four **difficult** aspects of Jesus' early childhood.

1. Jesus was ignored by His own people, even those who claimed to be experts on God, and was appreciated only by outsiders.

- In Matthew 2:4, who did Herod assemble to discover the birthplace of the Christ?

- What was their answer? (vv. 5-6)

- We have no indication that these "experts" of God went in search of Jesus. They knew the right answers, and that was apparently all that mattered to them. How might this speak a warning into our lives today?

- Meanwhile, in Matthew 2:1, *"wise men"* came to Jerusalem from where?

The old region of Babylon and Persia was located east of Jerusalem. And *"wise men"* is an interesting term. The Greek word *magoi* had a mysterious connotation. It was associated with magic, the study of sacred writings and astrology.

These were gentile (non-Jewish) men. We even have reason to think they were practicing "magic" contrary to God's law. And yet … God reached out to them and met them right where they were.

- What was the reaction of these men when finding Jesus? (Matthew 2:10-11)

- Have you ever questioned someone's experience with the Lord because it didn't look exactly like you would expect? Why or why not?

- Read 1 Samuel 16:7. How might this verse apply to the wise men?

2. Jesus became a refugee.

- What command did the angel give Joseph in Matthew 2:13?

- What thoughts come to your mind when you imagine our God as a tiny baby, His parents running for His life?

3. Jesus was threatened by those in power, and innocent people died.
- What was Herod's reaction, both emotional and physical, to the news that the wise men had evaded him? (Matthew 2:16)

Based on population estimates for this time in history, scholars estimate 10-30 babies were killed.
- Think of a time when someone's actions caused other people pain. It is not easy living in this fallen and broken world. Pray for anyone you know is experiencing that pain right now.

4. Jesus grew up despised.
- Matthew 2:23 says Jesus returned from Egypt and grew up in Nazareth. Read John 1:46. What did people think of Nazareth?

- What prophecy did Isaiah 53:3 give of the Messiah?

From the outside, none of this seems fair. Mary and Joseph had already been through so much. They were faithful followers of God, doing their best. And it was HARD. But friends, sometimes the hard place is exactly where God wants us. Because every hard moment in Matthew 2 was prophesied. It was predestined to fulfill God's plan.
- Pick one of the following verses of the Old Testament. How did the life of Jesus fulfill this prophecy? (Micah 5:2; Isaiah 60:1-6; Hosea 11:1; Jeremiah 31:15; Isaiah 53:3)

- What can you do today to trust God in the hard areas you face?

WEEK 1 / DAY 4

Matthew 3

MAJOR MOMENT
John the Baptizer baptized Jesus, and the Trinity rejoiced.

Thirty years passed between Matthew 2:23 and Matthew 3:1. Very little is known about those years in Jesus' life.
- What small insight does Luke give into Jesus' childhood/adolescence in Luke 2:40?

Before any of the events in Matthew took place, there was a period of God's silence. This one had lasted 400 years. Some of the last words of the last book of the Old Testament record an important prophecy.
- What does Malachi 4:5 say?

The end. For 400 years. And then we meet John the Baptizer in Matthew 3.
- According to Matthew 3:4, how did John dress?

- How does 2 Kings 1:8 describe the prophet Elijah's wardrobe?

- According to Matthew 3:1, where did John live?

  _____
  _____

- What prophecy is given in Isaiah 40:3?

  _____
  _____
  _____
  _____

John was to be a sign to the people, preparing the way of the Lord.

- What was John's message? (Matthew 3:2)

  _____
  _____
  _____
  _____

- In verse 10, John talked about trees bearing fruit. How does this verse relate to his message of repentance, and what might that teach us?

  _____
  _____
  _____
  _____

Then, in verse 13, Jesus walked onto the scene to be baptized. However, John's baptism was for repentance, and Jesus had no sin for which to repent!

- What reason does Jesus give for His baptism in verse 15?

  _____
  _____
  _____
  _____

- Second Corinthians 5:21 says, "[God] made him to be sin who knew no sin, so that in him _____ might become the _____ of God."

Jesus had no sin, but He took on ours on the cross and, in turn, gave us His righteousness. The baptism of Jesus was symbolic of what He came to accomplish. Going underneath the water and coming back up to life showed Jesus' coming death, burial and resurrection.

- What are you reminded of today in regard to Jesus' mission? Why did He come? Who did He come for?

Matthew 3:16-17 is one of the most beautiful images of the Trinity: one God who is Father, Son and Holy Spirit.
- In verse 16, who descended on Jesus and rested on Him?

- In verse 17, who spoke from heaven? What did He say?

Friend, if you have put your trust in Jesus and given Him your life, you are also a child of God. (2 Corinthians 6:18; 2 Corinthians 5:21; Romans 8:30; Psalm 147:11)
- Who, then, has descended and rests on you? (John 14:26; Romans 8:9; Ephesians 1:13)

- Who speaks from heaven over you? And what does He say? (Zephaniah 3:17)

Jesus came to this world for you and me. Every action had meaning. He chose to do it so that we could have a better life ... an eternal life. He hands us the reward and victory that belong to Him. What a gift. What a Savior.
- Take a moment to write down your thoughts, prayers or praise.

WEEK 1 / DAY 5

MAJOR MOMENT

Jesus resisted temptation and began His ministry.

Immediately following His baptism, Jesus headed into the wilderness to be tempted. Today's look at this temptation is going to offer a rich understanding of our sin nature and what lies at the heart of sin.

- In Matthew 4:3, the devil tempted a hungry Jesus by suggesting He do what?

- In Genesis 3:1, the devil tempted Eve to do what?

Both temptations involved eating something against God's will. And at the heart of both temptations was a questioning of God. For Eve, Satan suggested that God was holding out on her and Adam. To Jesus, he suggested the same, implying, "Why would God allow His own Son to be out here starving? Why is He not providing for You?" We, too, are tempted by what pastor David Platt calls the temptation of self-gratification: "We are tempted to fulfill our wants apart from God's will."[1]

- We all have desires (which are not necessarily wrong!). We need food, sleep and relationships. We want love and peace, just to name a few. Yet in what ways are we tempted to fulfill these desires apart from God's will?

- Jesus answered Satan in verse 4 by essentially saying that the "food" of God is better and more satisfying than bread. What does this mean? How does remembering this help us when we are tempted to fulfill our wants and needs our own way?

Let's look at the second temptation.
- According to Matthew 4:5-6, what did the devil tempt Jesus with here?

- Platt calls this the temptation of self-protection: "We are tempted to question God's presence and manipulate God's promises."[2] Why might we be tempted to twist God's Word to our liking? Why do you think we are so eager for "signs" God is still with us?

- Jesus' answer in verse 7 was simple. Essentially, He said He would trust God was present, no matter what. On days when it is hard to see or feel God's presence, why is it so important to have this faith in place?

Next let's break down the final temptation.
- According to Matthew 4:8-9, what did Satan offer and at what cost?

- Platt calls this the temptation of self-exaltation: "We are tempted to assert ourselves in the world while we rob God of His worship."[3] Satan offered Jesus the world, and in his offer, Jesus wouldn't have to suffer and die. He could have it all now. When have you been tempted to take "shortcuts" on God's plans?

- This would not be the last time Satan would tempt Jesus to abandon the cross. (See Matthew 16:23.) Yet Jesus always resisted. Bible scholar Russell Moore says, "Jesus refused to exchange the end-time exaltation by the Father for a right-now exaltation of a snake."[4] How can this thought apply to your life as well?

Jesus did what no other person in history could. He successfully resisted the heart of all temptations. Not once did He question God's presence, provision and power.
- What can you learn from Jesus to successfully resist temptation in your own life today?

Throughout our study of Matthew, we are going to look to the life of Jesus as a guide toward peace. The world we live in will nitpick our hearts and minds, dragging us down into chaos if we let it. To live a better way, Jesus' way, we have to be intentional on the path we choose.

Each weekend we are going to take a stop along Jesus' guide toward peace to learn what this path looks like and how we can stay on it. We will build on this path as we go along, so you will have a full path to reference by the end. This weekend, let's make our first stop.

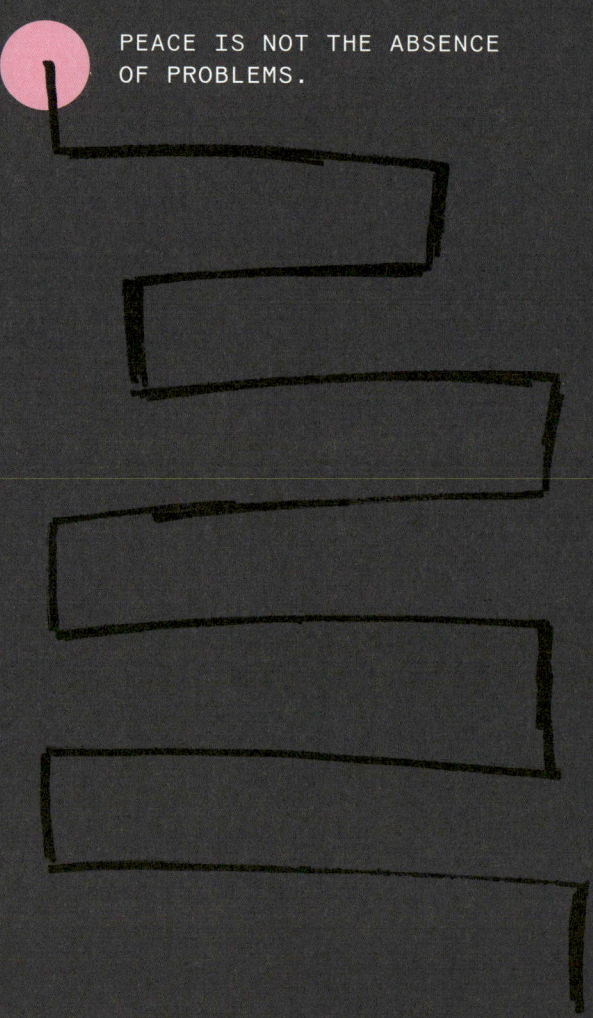

PEACE IS NOT THE ABSENCE OF PROBLEMS.

Weekend Reflection

Peace is not the absence of problems.

Did you see much peace in our first five days of study? I mean, the writer of Psalm 89 had questions about God's faithfulness. Jesus' family line and the history of Israel were filled with chaotic events and disappointing characters. Jesus' birth and early childhood were jam-packed with difficulties. When we saw Jesus at His baptism, His life was already echoing His path toward death. And then He was tempted with the very heart of all temptations. We indeed see the *frenzy* of the world ... but peace?

However, the beginning of Jesus' life and ministry provides us with our first important truth about peace. **Peace is not the absence of problems.** Are you struggling with family or finances? Does your life not look like you thought it would or should when you reached this age? Are the voices in your head loud, negative and full of lies? Life is just plain hard sometimes. And somewhere along the way, maybe you were taught that peace would mean no more conflict or pain or struggle. But Jesus' life speaks something different.

In John 14:27, Jesus said, *"Peace I leave with you; my peace I give to you. Not as the world gives do I give to you. Let not your hearts be troubled, neither let them be afraid."* Jesus had peace in the midst of problems. He wasn't troubled by or afraid of them. And He offers that peace to you as well.

Don't let life's troubles throw you off-course. Even in the midst of the hard, you can still walk the path of peace. Just keep your eyes on Jesus.

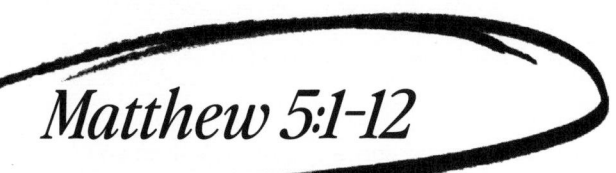

Matthew 5:1-12

WEEK 2 / DAY 6

MAJOR MOMENT
Jesus began His Sermon on the Mount with the Beatitudes.

Matthew 5-7 is what is known as the Sermon on the Mount. In this sermon, which we will cover in the next several days, Jesus gives many guidelines for living. And while these provide us with what it looks like to live a better way, they may not be what we expect when we think of living in God's blessings. Today we are going to start with the Beatitudes, which are a set of eight *"Blessed are ..."* statements. The word "blessed" here means having divine joy and perfect happiness.[1]

- Before we begin, what do you think of when you imagine divine joy and perfect happiness? What comes to mind, or what is something you feel you would need in order to experience this?

Blessed Are the Poor in Spirit (Matthew 5:3)
- This term refers to those who recognize they are in need of God's help. They cry out, "God, I can't do this on my own." What most recent circumstance in your life has caused you to cry out to God for help? Did you consider this position a blessing at the time? Why or why not?

Blessed Are Those Who Mourn (Matthew 5:4)
- Mourning implies a sense of brokenness and sorrow. It is to feel the weight of sin and its consequences in our lives and in the world. What areas of sin and death cause you to mourn today?

Blessed Are the Meek (Matthew 5:5)
- Meekness means humility and gentleness. It is about recognizing God's authority and power to take care of you. What area of life might you be grasping, trying to control in your own power, that you instead need to humbly and gently let go and hand over to God?

Blessed Are Those Who Hunger and Thirst for Righteousness (Matthew 5:6)
- We have innate cravings within us. Unfortunately, we often look to worldly fixes to satisfy us. These "fixes" can be food, drink, possessions, careers or any other ways we fill in this blank: *If I just had _____, then I would be happy.* What is it that you occasionally try to fill in that blank with? If we know true righteousness is only found in God, then what (or who) is verse 6 saying we should crave (because He is the only One who can truly satisfy)?

Blessed Are the Merciful (Matthew 5:7)
- I think of the Beatitudes as being like a tree, each verse a new branch of growth in our character development. So far, we have talked about needing God, being broken over sin, humbly submitting to God and desiring only Him. After God satisfies our thirsty souls with His mercy and love, why does it only make sense that this next verse asks us to be merciful to others?

Blessed Are the Pure in Heart (Matthew 5:8)
- Jewish leaders during Jesus' time were consumed with outward purity rituals. They washed religiously, wore special garments and only ate certain foods. But what is Jesus concerned with in verse 8, and how is it different from ritual purity?

Blessed Are the Peacemakers (Matthew 5:9)
- Peacemakers have an ability to sense conflict and a desire to help resolve it. However, lasting peace can only come when a person's heart is right with God. With that in mind, what do peacemakers help others do?

Blessed Are the Persecuted (Matthew 5:10-12)
- This means staying true to God, no matter the cost. Has it ever cost you something to follow Jesus? Why or why not?

To end today, take a quick look back over the Beatitudes.
- Would you say the world would agree with Jesus that these eight traits are blessings, resulting in divine joy and perfect happiness? Why or why not?

WEEK 2 / DAY 7

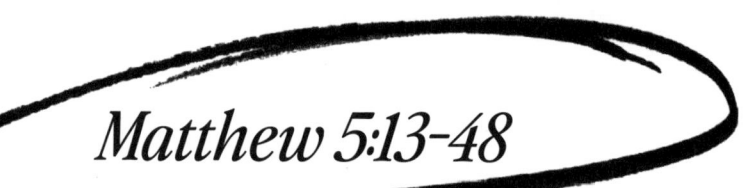
Matthew 5:13-48

MAJOR MOMENT
Jesus fulfilled the law and explained that sin is a heart issue.

There is something satisfying about having tangible tasks written down and being able to check off a list. In some ways, many people see the Ten Commandments as a sort of checklist. Do (or don't do) these 10 things, and perhaps that makes you good with God. However, Jesus explained that the Law of the Old Testament was never about having a checklist.

- Think for a moment about a checklist. How do you feel when you have completed your tasks? In most cases, who does all the work?

_____
_____
_____
_____

The problem with viewing the Old Testament, or even the New Testament, as a checklist to follow is that it leaves the work to us. We have to accomplish the tasks by our own work. And we can't. Let's look at the examples Jesus gives from the Old Testament …

- In Matthew 5:21 Jesus mentions murder. We all know this to be a sin. Yet according to Jesus in Matthew 5:22, what seemingly "lesser" sin is also condemned?

_____
_____
_____
_____

- In Matthew 5:27 Jesus mentions adultery, another well-known sin. Yet according to Matthew 5:28, what seemingly "lesser" sin is also condemned?

_____
_____
_____
_____

- The divorce certificate mentioned in Matthew 5:31 was an easily accessible bill of divorce a person could obtain for any reason. It reflected the fact that divorce and remarriage were widely accepted and practiced in the first-century world.[1] What sin issues might have been at the heart of these easily accessible divorces?

- Matthew 5:33 mentions swearing by oaths. Swearing by God's name or any substitute was the only way to "guarantee" that what a person said was true. Why specifically do you think we sometimes lie?

- The law about "an eye for an eye" mentioned in Matthew 5:38 was established by God (Leviticus 24:20) as a safety rule for society. This was meant to ensure someone was not punished unfairly (for example, a death sentence for stealing a loaf of bread). However, human nature twists this law to support our desire for revenge. What are perhaps the heart issues behind revenge?

- Funnily, in Matthew 5:43 Jesus said, *"You have heard that it was said, 'You shall love your neighbor and hate your enemy.'"* Actually, nowhere in the Old Testament does it ever say "hate your enemy." This was something people added through the years. How would you define the word "enemy," and what might it look like to love this kind of person? (v. 44)

Let's look these over and draw some conclusions.

- According to Jesus' standards, the "checklist" mentality becomes much more difficult. Have you ever been angry? Had an impure thought? Acted selfishly? Told a lie? Wanted to hurt someone who hurt you? When was the last time you asked God to richly bless someone who wanted to see you fail? How's your "checklist"?

- Jesus said every commandment had to be kept, not just to the letter of the law but the spirit of the law, too. And I think you and I both know … we could never do it. The law is not a checklist we can keep but rather a means of awareness of our need for a Savior who can keep it. What did Jesus say He came to do in Matthew 5:17? And what does that mean for you and me?

WEEK 2 / DAY 8

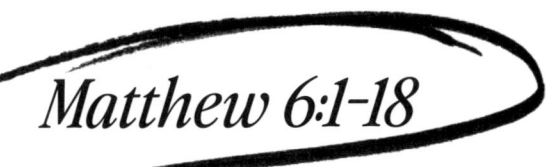

MAJOR MOMENT
Jesus taught that motive matters.

Yesterday we learned that, just as much as external actions, God is concerned about the condition of our hearts. This is where sin is rooted. Today we will see even our GOOD actions can be stumbling blocks if our hearts are not in the right place.

GIVING
- In Matthew 6:2, Jesus warned against giving for the wrong reason. What was this wrong reason?

The reality is that it is difficult to give without expecting anything in return. This can be so subtle. Sometimes when I've given, my motive has been to know the recipient was grateful or appreciative. I wanted thanks. Sometimes I've given and then wanted to tell people HOW to use the gift. My motive has been control. Sometimes I've given, and my motivation has been that God would in some way reward me, whether physically or even with a good, smooth day. I wanted God's favor. All these motives are wrong, but how sneaky they can be!
- What sneaky wrong motives have you seen try to creep into your giving?

PRAYER
- In Matthew 6:5-7, what two things does Jesus warn against in prayer?

There is a time and place for public prayer, as well as a time and place for guided or memorized prayer. However, when Jesus gave us what is known to many as the Lord's Prayer, He said, *"Pray then like this..."* (Matthew 6:9, emphasis mine). The Greek word *(houtō)* means "in this manner." In other words, Jesus gave us a pattern to follow. Use the table below to conduct your own prayer today, following the pattern of Matthew 6:9-13

THE LORD'S PRAYER	THE MAIN IDEA	YOUR PRAYER
Our Father in heaven, hallowed be your name.	Offer worship and praise to our Father.	
Your kingdom come, your will be done, on earth as it is in heaven.	Submit to God's will, and pray for His Kingdom.	
Give us this day our daily bread ...	Pray for daily provisions, and recognize all we have is from Him.	
and forgive us our debts, as we also have forgiven our debtors.	Ask the Holy Spirit to show us our sin, lead us to repentance and give us hearts of mercy.	
And lead us not into temptation, but deliver us from evil.	Pray for protection and guidance to keep us in His will.	

FASTING

Interestingly, God had required Jewish people to fast once a year on the Day of Atonement. (Leviticus 23:27) However, Pharisees of this time were proudly and publicly fasting twice a week! (Luke 18:12) Super holy, right?[1]

- How did Jesus describe the hypocrites' fasting in Matthew 6:16?

WHAT WE LEARN:

The world tries to tell us it's cool to shout about our good deeds, letting everyone know what awesome people we are. It says we need to be able to impress people with our eloquent speech and persuasive arguments; we should work harder and be better than the rest. Is that mentality wearing you out? Let's look at Jesus' way ...

- In Matthew 6:4, Jesus says our giving should be done in what? Verse 6 says to pray to *"your Father who is in"* what? Verse 18b says in fasting, your Father sees in what?

- There is only one place where we can truly cultivate the heart. Only one place where character is more important than reputation. That is in the quiet, secret place of your life that only God sees. How can you focus on that place this week?

WEEK 2 / DAY 9

Matthew 6:19-34

MAJOR MOMENT

Jesus taught about treasure.

I once heard someone say they knew exactly how much money you need to be happy. The answer? "A little more than you have today." Then repeat that scenario every day of your life. It certainly says something about our desire to want more. Forbes.com wrote an article back in 2017 saying it was estimated that people were exposed to 4,000 to 10,000 advertisements each DAY.[1] That many messages trying to tell us something else we "need"?! The Toy Industry Association did research that found the average child in the U.S. received more than $6,500 worth of toys before they became a teenager.[2] And yet are those children happier for it? Or is this one more example of how the world tries to steal our sanity? Today, let's look at a better way.

- According to Matthew 6:19, what can happen to earthly treasure?

- My dad can remember his mom always saying, "The more stuff you have, the more stuff you have to take care of." In what ways does earthly treasure take from our time, energy, resources and sanity?

- Read Matthew 6:20. What might *"treasures in heaven"* look like? List some here.

Bible scholar Warren Wiersbe says, "It is not wrong to possess things, but it is wrong for things to possess us."[3] Matthew 6:21 speaks about the heart. Verses 22-23 speak about the "eye," which is synonymous with the mind in ancient Near Eastern symbolism.[4] Verse 24 speaks about our will, or who we will serve. Our hearts, minds and wills can be spent serving "stuff" or God.

- Just take a quick evaluation of your life: Who or what gets the most attention in your heart, mind and will right now? How is this affecting your peace?

If you are like me, you are sensing the struggle. All of the modern conveniences that are supposed to make my life easier, all the possessions (or lack of possessions), the items in my online "cart" that I expect to be delivered in two days (or items stuck on my "wish list" that I long to afford), aren't making my life more peaceful. They are increasing my anxiety.

- What does Jesus say in Matthew 6:25, 6:31 and 6:34?

- How does Jesus say we are to do this, according to verse 33?

- What does Romans 8:32 say?

- What does Philippians 4:6 say? And what does Philippians 4:7 add that we will then have?

- Looking at all these verses, what is the key to fighting off what I call my "want monster"? In other words, what is going to help us when we feel that anxiety over needing and wanting more and more?

- Summarize what you learned today in one sentence.

WEEK 2 / DAY 10

Matthew 7

MAJOR MOMENT

Jesus shared the importance of discernment.

Today we will be looking at the final chapter of Jesus' Sermon on the Mount. This section deals with discernment, or what you might call "judgment," for both others and ourselves. Let's jump in.

- Matthew 7:1 says what?

- The tense of the Greek verb for "judged" in verse 1 signifies a once-for-all, final judgment. Essentially, it means "to play God."[1] What do you think this kind of judging looks like today?

- Jesus is not saying we should never evaluate other people's behaviors. There is a time and place for helping *"take the speck out of your brother's eye."* But before we can correctly do so, what must take place first? (v. 5)

- Dogs and pigs, mentioned in verse 6, were wild scavengers during this time period, known to attack anyone who might have food. When might be a time in ministry when we need to discern wisely where and when to share the "pearls" of the gospel?

Goodness, these are difficult commands. We have to be so careful how we judge people. We have to be constantly aware of our own state of sin and need for Jesus. How will we correctly discern when to save even right judgments for a later moment? Jesus tells us ...

- What is His command in Matthew 7:7?

- What specifically does James 1:5 tell us to ask for?

- What other idea does Jesus give us in Matthew 7:12 that will guide us as we interact with others?

There is a reason we need God's help and wisdom in discerning both with others and in ourselves.

- 1 Samuel 16:7 gives us some insight into this. We mentioned this important verse when discussing the wise men on Day 3. Do you remember what it says?

- Let's use this to break down these last sections. From the outside, what might false teachers look like? (Matthew 7:15)

- We also cannot always judge a fruit tree by its outward appearance. What instead must we wait and watch for? (v. 20)

- From the outside, what will some people appear to believe about God, and yet still they will be rejected by the Lord? (vv. 21-23)

- From the outside, two houses might look identical. Yet what is the difference? (vv. 24-27)

- What are we reminded of from these sections, both when it comes to examining others and our own lives?

So much of what we looked at today involves the condition of our own hearts. We cannot help others if we are blind to our own sin. Without God's wisdom, we cannot know who is open to receive the gospel. We cannot pronounce a final, eternal judgment on any life because we realize all we can see is the outside. To live like Jesus, in a better way, is to change the way we see. We first look at ourselves before turning a critical eye on others. We don't measure others by worldly standards but by the grace of Jesus that we ourselves have tasted and seen.

- What words from Jesus are speaking to your heart today?

Each weekend we are taking a stop along Jesus' guide toward peace. This weekend, let's arrive at our second stop.

Weekend Reflection

Peace cannot be manufactured.

This week we talked a lot about the heart. Matthew 5:8 says, *"Blessed are the pure in heart, for they shall see God."* I can think of no greater peace than to see God Himself. But I also know that it is not possible, apart from a miracle of God, to be *"pure in heart."* This involves having to dig up the very roots that grow under sin. This looks like doing everything with the right motives and growing our hearts in the secret, quiet places no one sees. This means watering our love for treasure in heaven and starving the "want monster" inside of us. This is about realizing outside appearances mean little, and what matters is the fruit that takes time and patience to find.

Friends, none of this we can do on our own. Oh, we can try. We can work hard to improve our heart condition, but in the end, it will not hold. The truth is, I don't need a better me … I need a NEW me. And only Jesus Christ can create a new me. Only in Jesus can I crucify my old self and receive a flood of mercy and grace. Only the Spirit of Jesus can produce the good fruit I desire to have. Which tells me something about peace. **Peace cannot be manufactured.** I can strive and work and try my best, but deep down I know I am disillusioned to think I can somehow create lasting peace. Real peace is a fruit of the Spirit, planted by Jesus, that He alone can make grow in me.

Does this mean I throw up my hands and do whatever I want, hoping peace will catch up to me sooner or later? As Paul would say, *"By no means!"* (Romans 6:2). We can approach every day as an opportunity to walk by Jesus' side, participating in the amazing work He is doing inside us.

Are you worn out from trying to create perfect, lasting peace in your life? Maybe it is time to let go. We cannot manufacture peace. But we can stay in step with Jesus and watch Him work in our hearts. And one day we will look up to realize today we had a little more peace than yesterday, and it is all because of Him.

Psalm 37

WEEK 3 / DAY 11

MAJOR MOMENT
The meek shall inherit the land.

Today we are going to take a quick detour back to the psalms. Last week's study of the Sermon on the Mount has set us up perfectly to discover new depths in Psalm 37. Psalm 37 is known as a "wisdom psalm" because it is a hymn meant to teach and encourage God's people. To begin today, let's compare some of the verses in Psalm 37 to teachings Jesus gave in the Sermon on the Mount. It will help to have both Psalm 37 and Matthew 5-7 open or bookmarked.

- What does Psalm 37:4 say, and how does that relate to Matthew 6:33?

- What does Psalm 37:11 say, and how does that relate to Matthew 5:5?

- What does Psalm 37:20 say, and how does that relate to Matthew 6:30?

- What does Psalm 37:35-36 say, and how does that relate to Matthew 7:19?

- Look carefully through Psalm 37. What other verses do you find that remind you of a teaching of Jesus from His Sermon on the Mount?

Let's set our focus today specifically on Psalm 37:11.
- Psalm 37:11 specifically says that who shall inherit the land?

- We can get a glimpse into what this word means by looking up at verse 9. This verse says those who do what shall inherit the land?

Bible Scholar Derek Kidner says in his commentary on Psalm, "The context gives the best possible definition of *the meek*: they are those who choose the way of patient faith instead of self-assertion."[1]
- What does that mean to you?

To me, that says I do not have to constantly prove myself to others. I also don't have to fight everyone I meet to make sure I get what I "deserve" or "my fair share." In fact, meekness frees me from focusing on myself all the time and allows me to put that focus elsewhere. Namely, on the Lord.
- These verses say the meek shall _____ the land. What does this word mean? What work do you have to do to inherit something?

To inherit something, I only have to be in a person's will. God says when we stop trying to look out for ourselves all the time, He will simply give us the land. In other words, He will take care of us. He will provide. He has a plan. And when we know and believe and trust in that truth, then something wonderful happens.

- According to Psalm 37:11, a meek person will *"delight themselves in"* what?

　

- Why do you think that might be the reward of meekness?

WEEK 3 / DAY 12

Matthew 8

MAJOR MOMENT

Jesus demonstrated His authority.

Before we look at Matthew 8 today, let's take a quick glance back at where we left off in Matthew 7.
- According to Matthew 7:28-29, why were the crowds astonished after Jesus taught the Sermon on the Mount?

From the beginning, something was different about Jesus. He had an authority no other man had ever shown. Matthew strategically sets up Chapters 8 and 9 to demonstrate this power and authority of Jesus. I like how Bible scholar David Platt refers to Chapter 8 as testifying to Jesus' power over the four D's: disease, disciples, disaster and demons.[1]

DISEASE
- Who did Jesus heal in Matthew 8:2-3? How about in verses 5-13? And who specifically in verses 14-15?

- I love that Matthew intentionally brings out examples of Jesus' healing, and he does so by highlighting Jesus' love for those marginalized or disdained by others. Lepers were outcasts in this society. Roman armies were hated. Servants were treated as property, and women were disregarded. Yet these are the very people Jesus ministered to. What might this teach us?

- Jesus showed His authority over disease. He is more powerful than leprosy, paralysis, viruses and infection. He is more powerful than chronic illness, cancer and diabetes. What physical ailments are on your heart and mind such that you need the reminder that Jesus is more powerful?

- Jesus' life on earth was a foretaste of His future Kingdom. Today, we still have disease. We are not guaranteed physical healing in this life. But we do have the hope and truth and peace that come from knowing someday at Jesus' return, and in eternity, He will exercise His power over disease FOREVER. Read Revelation 21:4. What does that mean to you?

DISCIPLES
- Of what did Jesus warn the scribe who wanted to follow Him in Matthew 8:20?

- What did Jesus tell the disciple who wanted to first bury his father? (v. 22) (Note: Some scholars suggest that, because burials were often held the same day as death during this time, this disciple was asking to wait until his father died, perhaps to receive his inheritance.[1])

- Jesus has authority over our will. He has the right to ask us to do something that is **uncomfortable** or **inconvenient** to us at the time. Do you see that in your own life? Why or why not?

DISASTER

- How did Jesus demonstrate His authority over all creation in Matthew 8:23-27?

  _____
  _____
  _____
  _____

- Read Job 38:8-12. What are you reminded about God's power?

  _____
  _____
  _____
  _____

DEMONS

- Jesus also had an interesting encounter that demonstrated His authority over demons. In Matthew 8:29, demons cried out, *"What have you to do with us, O Son of God? Have you come here to torment us _____ _____ _____?"*

- When Jesus said, *"Go,"* what did the demons have to do? (v. 32)

  _____
  _____
  _____
  _____

Looking over these examples of Jesus' great authority and power ...

- What is your answer to the disciples' question: *"What sort of man is this"* (v. 27)?

  _____
  _____
  _____
  _____
  _____
  _____

Miracles of Jesus
(as recorded in Matthew)

Healed a man from leprosy	MATTHEW 8:1-4
Healed centurion's servant	MATTHEW 8:5-13
Healed Peter's mother-in-law	MATTHEW 8:14-15
Cast out demons and healed many sick	MATTHEW 8:16-17
Calmed a storm	MATTHEW 8:23-27
Cast out demons from two men into a herd of pigs	MATTHEW 8:28-34
Healed a paralytic man	MATTHEW 9:1-8
Healed a bleeding woman	MATTHEW 9:20-22
Restored life to a ruler's daughter	MATTHEW 9:18-26
Healed two blind men	MATTHEW 9:27-31
Healed a man unable to speak	MATTHEW 9:32-34
Healed a man with a withered hand	MATTHEW 12:9-14
Healed a blind, mute man who was demon-oppressed	MATTHEW 12:22-23
Fed 5,000 with five loaves and two fish	MATTHEW 14:13-21
Walked on water	MATTHEW 14:22-23
Healed many sick in Gennesaret	MATTHEW 14:34-36
Healed Canaanite woman's demon-oppressed daughter	MATTHEW 15:21-28
Fed 4,000 with seven loaves and a few fish	MATTHEW 15:32-39
Healed a demon-oppressed boy	MATTHEW 17:14-20
Caused temple tax to be found in a fish's mouth	MATTHEW 17:24-27
Healed two more blind men	MATTHEW 20:29-34
Caused fig tree to wither	MATTHEW 21:18-22

Look over this list of miracles. Jesus healed men and women, young and old, rich and poor, Jew and gentile. Jesus had authority over sickness, death, oppression and creation.

What does seeing this list teach you about Jesus?

WEEK 3 / DAY 13

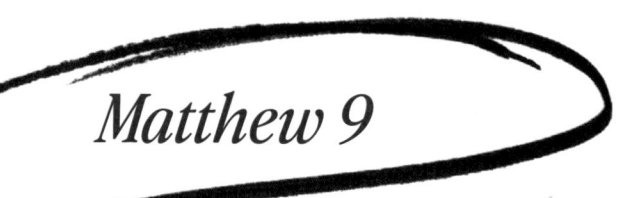
Matthew 9

MAJOR MOMENT

Jesus had authority over sin and death because Jesus is God.

Yesterday we briefly mentioned that Matthew, with the Holy Spirit's inspiration, strategically set up Chapters 8 and 9 to demonstrate the power and authority of Jesus. Chapter 8 shows how Jesus has authority over disease, disciples, disaster and demons. However, these were only touching the surface of the real problem over which Jesus has authority. In Chapter 9, Matthew points out that Jesus also has authority over sin and death because Jesus is God.

SIN

- When Jesus encountered the paralytic man, what shocking thing did He first tell this man in Matthew 9:2?

In verse 3, the scribes claimed this to be blaspheming. "Blaspheming" means doing something to degrade or insult God. According to the scribes, Jesus blasphemed by claiming to forgive sins, which only God can forgive.

- Therefore, by making this statement, Jesus was claiming to be who?

To show He had power over both body and soul, Jesus secondly healed the man's body. However, the order of these miracles does send the message that our ultimate need is not physical; it's spiritual.[1]

- What does that sentence mean to you, and where might it apply in your life?

- To demonstrate Jesus' ability to save sinners, Matthew also offered up his own testimony. According to Matthew 9:9, as a reminder, what was Matthew's former career? According to verse 10, who were his friends who came to meet Jesus?

_____
_____
_____

In Matthew 9:14, John's disciples coming to ask about fasting might seem random, but it's not. We may fast occasionally today for certain reasons, but fasting was an even bigger part of the old way, the old covenant. The old covenant also included a system of sacrifices continually offered to forgive sin. Jesus was ushering in a new way. A better way.

- Read Hebrews 9:12 and verse 15. How is Jesus' new covenant better?

_____
_____
_____

DEATH

- As human beings, truly our greatest struggles are against sin and against something else we see in Matthew 9:18. What happened to the ruler's daughter?

_____
_____
_____

Before we see what happens with this daughter, Jesus is interrupted by a woman who had been bleeding for 12 years. Under Levitical law, she would have been unclean, separated from temple worship and from her friends and family, who she could also make unclean just by touching.

- Therefore, Jesus' healing not only healed her body but also allowed her what?

_____
_____
_____

Jesus demonstrated He had authority even over death by taking the hand of the girl and bringing her back to life. (Matthew 9:24-25) Amazing! Under Old Testament law, touching a bleeding woman or touching a dead body made the person who touched them instantly unclean. But not Jesus. Jesus is

the One who instead MAKES CLEAN those who are not.
- How is this a beautiful picture of our redemption?

Jesus had, and has, power and authority over sin and death! How is He able to do this? Matthew places key miracles at the end of Chapter 9 to show us.
- Isaiah 35:5-6 was a well-known prophecy about the coming Messiah. Read these verses and then read Matthew 9:27-33. What is Matthew trying to show?

- In what ways does seeing Jesus' authority over sin and death guide us toward peace?

WEEK 3 / DAY 14

MAJOR MOMENT

Jesus called His disciples and gave instructions for both then and now.

The end of Matthew 9 leads us so beautifully into today's look at Chapter 10.
- In Matthew 9:36, what was Jesus feeling, and why?

- In verse 38, what did Jesus say we should do for the harassed and helpless?

To demonstrate that answer, Matthew transitions into Jesus calling His 12 disciples. Find "The 12 Disciples" chart on page 68 in your study guide to learn more about these men. These 12 had different personalities, different occupations and varying social/economic positions and academic backgrounds, yet together they would send the message of Christ into the world.
- What do the differences among the disciples remind you about the Church? What might it remind you about your place in God's family?

Next, Jesus gives out instructions. It is important when breaking down Chapter 10 to realize that verses 5-15 were given to the 12 disciples for their particular short-term mission. The verses after are general statements regarding the long-term mission we all have to bring the gospel to the world. Let's look first at this short-term mission.

- Jesus' command to His disciples in Matthew 10:5-6 might seem confusing. He told them, *"Go nowhere among the Gentiles ... but go rather to the lost sheep of the house of Israel"* (vv. 5-6). Israel was the chosen nation of God and therefore was given the first opportunity to see and understand Jesus' bigger mission. What does Paul say in Acts 13:46? What about Romans 1:16?

Let's now move on to the instructions for the long-term mission that affects us all.

- What are your feelings toward comfort? Safety? Maybe even "world peace"? (If you are like me, you like them ... a lot!)

- Looking through Matthew 10:16-25, what did Jesus say were some of the things His followers could expect?

- I love Jesus' advice in verse 16 to be *"wise as serpents and innocent as doves."* Friends, this world is dangerous, and we need to be smart but also humble and kind. I think of it as wisdom under restraint. What do Jesus' words mean to you?

In this study we are looking deeply at peace.

- Write down the words from Matthew 10:34.

    _____
    _____
    _____
    _____

- That is a tough sentence to swallow. Look at the following verses from throughout Chapter 10 and write down different groups of people we could possibly NOT have peace with on earth: verses 17-18, 21, 35-36.

    _____
    _____
    _____
    _____

- Jesus, the Prince of Peace, (Isaiah 9:6) said He did not come to bring peace to the earth. According to Matthew 10:28, who should we fear, and why? Therefore, Jesus' main goal was not to bring us peace here on earth, with other people, but to bring us peace with who?

    _____
    _____
    _____
    _____
    _____

- God knows the number of hairs on your head. (Matthew 10:30) He knows the movement and life of every tiny baby bird and more surely knows your movements and life. (v. 31) Your eternity is in His hand, and no one — NO ONE — can take that away from you. (v. 32) How does knowing all this bring you peace?

    _____
    _____
    _____
    _____
    _____

The 12 Disciples of Jesus

Disciple's Known Names (It was common during this time period to have more than one name.)	What We Know
Peter (Simon, Simon Peter)	A fisherman, portrayed as a man who spoke his mind and often acted impulsively.
Andrew	Peter's brother, also a fisherman. Andrew was first a follower of John the Baptist before convincing Peter to join him in following Jesus. (John 1:35-40)
James, son of Zebedee (James the Greater)	A fisherman. Jesus called him and his brother John "sons of thunder." James was also the first apostle to be martyred. (Acts 12:1-3)
John, son of Zebedee	Brother to James, also a fisherman. John wrote the Gospel of John, as well as 1 John, 2 John, 3 John and Revelation.
Philip	Came from Bethsaida by the Sea of Galilee (same as Peter and Andrew). He brought Nathanael (aka Bartholomew) to Jesus. (John 1:45)
Bartholomew (Nathanael)	An associate of Philip.
Thomas (Didymus, or the Twin)	The one many of us know as "Doubting Thomas" because he wanted proof before believing in Jesus' resurrection. (John 20:25)
Matthew (Levi)	A tax collector.
James, son of Alphaeus	To distinguish him from James, son of Zebedee, this James was sometimes called James the Younger. (Mark 15:40)
Thaddeus (Judas, son of James; Jude)	Little is known, though he did ask a question to Jesus in John 14:22.
Simon the Zealot	Zealots were political activists who often sought revolution as a means to free their nation from Roman oppression.
Judas Iscariot	Betrayed Jesus for 30 pieces of silver.

WEEK 3 / DAY 15

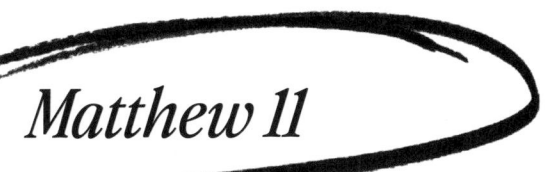
Matthew 11

MAJOR MOMENT

Jesus addressed doubt, unbelief and striving.

In Chapters 11-12, Matthew took a closer look at some of the opposition Jesus faced and His words toward it.

- Matthew 11 starts out with the prophet John the Baptist in prison, asking a question. What was that question? (v. 3)

_____
_____
_____
_____

Even John the Baptist, whom Jesus would later call the greatest born of women, (v. 11a) had doubts. When we look at John, we can see that his doubt arose from his own difficult circumstances, his confusion that Jesus did not meet all of his expectations of what the Messiah would be like, and his own inability to see and comprehend the bigger picture.[1]

- Think of a time when you struggled with doubt. Which of John's dilemmas listed above relate to your experience of doubt as well? In what ways?

_____
_____
_____
_____

- Notice that Jesus did not seem to be offended by John's question. Sit with that for a moment and write down your thoughts.

_____
_____
_____
_____
_____
_____

- Jesus offered an answer to John that speaks to us as well. Jesus directed him back to God's Word. Read Isaiah 35:5-6 and 61:1; then read Jesus' reply to John in Matthew 11:4-6. Why might these words have brought John peace? (In particular, focus on the first two lines of Isaiah 61:1.)

In Matthew 11:11, Jesus said *"among those born of women there has arisen no one greater than John the Baptist."* This title actually had little to do with John himself. John was the greatest because he was tasked with the greatest job: He was the prophet who got to announce the arrival of the King. Yet John would die before Jesus' Kingdom was established.

- What did Jesus say (the last sentence of Matthew 11:11) to us? And in what way is what we have in Jesus even better than what John got to see?

We have taken a look at doubt. Now we will look at something quite different: unbelief. Bible scholar Alister McGrath says, "Doubt arises within the context of faith. It is a wistful longing to be sure of the things in which we trust." In contrast, "Unbelief is the decision to live your life as if there is no God. It is a deliberate decision to reject Jesus Christ and all that he stands for."[2]

Jesus compared unbelief to the immature behavior of a child who refuses to play unless everyone follows her game (Matthew 11:16-17) and to the ignorance of rejecting a message because you don't like the messenger. (vv. 18-19) "Refusing" and "rejecting" are both words we are used to hearing associated with unbelief. Yet Jesus takes it a step further.

- In Matthew 11:20, Jesus denounced cities where what had been done? Yet what did they not do?

- To be indifferent means to have no particular interest in something. You do not see it as good or bad and remain unconcerned. After reading Matthew 11:20-24, do you believe a person can be indifferent toward Jesus? Why or why not?

When presented with Jesus, we have to make a choice. But sometimes the choice to have faith is hard. And Jesus tells us what to do then ...

- The religious leaders had been telling the people for centuries that they needed to DO more and try harder. But in Matthew 11:28, Jesus says, "_____ to me, all who labor and are heavy laden, and _____ will _____ you _____."

- Yoke is associated with work. Jesus says His yoke is *"easy"* (meaning "well-fitting") and *"light"* (v. 30). What does this mean to you? And how does that bring you peace today?

Friends, the world will try to tell us what peace looks like but will lead us astray. What does Jesus teach us about peace? This weekend, let's arrive at our third stop.

PEACE IS NOT THE ABSENCE OF PROBLEMS.

PEACE WITH GOD DOES NOT ALWAYS MEAN PEACE WITH OTHERS.

PEACE CANNOT BE MANUFACTURED.

Weekend Reflection

Peace with God does not always mean peace with others.

In Matthew 10:34a, Jesus said He did not come to bring *"peace to the earth."* He told us we would be *"hated by all for [His] name's sake"* (Matthew 10:22a). He reminded us that the way people treat the teacher is the way people will treat the student. (Matthew 10:24) Then Matthew 11-12 showed us how people treated the teacher. They rejected Him, judged Him or just plain ignored Him. We can expect the same treatment from the world.

This doesn't exactly feel like peace, does it? This feels like conflict and division. The global wish for "world peace" will not be coming true, at least not in this world. And that can feel discouraging if we stop there. However, Jesus doesn't stop there. He didn't come to bring perfect peace to the earth during His first visit, but peace can still be found by His people today. He has brought *"peace among those with whom he is pleased"* (Luke 2:14). And His is a greater and better form of peace. Jesus came to bring us peace with God. We have the peace of knowing eternal life with Him awaits us at His second coming.

So yes, **peace with God does not always mean peace with others.** Not everyone will like us or agree with us. Wars will continue to be fought. Families will break. Crime and injustice will keep taking place. But as followers of Jesus, we can still have peace. It is a peace inside of us, knowing we are loved and forgiven. It is knowing what the future holds and who holds the future. And until then, we live the words of Romans 12:18: *"If possible, so far as it depends on you, live peaceably with all."* And we leave the rest to Jesus.

WEEK 4 / DAY 16

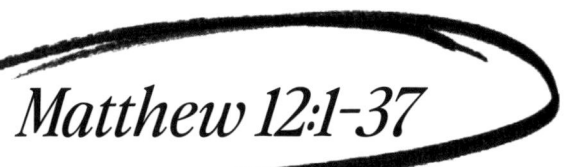
Matthew 12:1-37

MAJOR MOMENT

Opposition to Jesus continued to rise.

To begin today, let's take a quick look back at one of the last verses we studied in Matthew 11.

- In Matthew 11:28, Jesus says, *"Come to me, all who labor and are heavy laden, and …"* what?

- In today's reading of Matthew 12, the Pharisees were upset with Jesus in verses 2 and 10 because of what day?

The Greek word *sabat* means "rest." God had created Sabbath as a way for people to rest from their strivings. Yet the Pharisees in their legalism had turned Sabbath into a burden. Bible scholar Sam Storms defines legalism as "the tendency to regard as divine law things that God has neither required nor forbidden in Scripture, and the corresponding inclination to look with suspicion on others for their failure or refusal to conform."[1]

- After seeing the above definition, why might legalism be tempting, and why is it dangerous?

In Matthew 12:8, Jesus called Himself the *"lord of the Sabbath."*
- If Sabbath is meant to be a rest from works, in what way might Jesus be our ultimate Sabbath? (See Ephesians 2:8-9 and Romans 11:6.)

- How might this bring you peace today?

I find Matthew 12:15-21 so interesting. In all of His encounters with opposition so far, Jesus had strong, authoritative verbal answers for the Pharisees.
- Yet, according to verse 15, what was Jesus' reaction this time?

- Think of an argument or conflict you have had where there came a time to simply withdraw. Why might that be the appropriate response sometimes?

- I think we see a key part to Jesus' decision here when we read Matthew 12:14. What do you think may have been the condition of the Pharisees' hearts? What did they want to do?

This heart condition of the Pharisees is going to be vital to remember as we walk into this next section with the demon-oppressed man.

- When Jesus cast out the demon, from whom did the Pharisees say Jesus got His power? (v. 24)

The Pharisees knew the Scriptures better than anyone else (supposedly). They knew the prophecies of the Messiah. And they watched Jesus closely. They saw His numerous miracles, heard His authoritative words. Jesus showed He could answer every argument they gave. If anything, they should have been the first to bow before Him as their Lord. And yet, with everything they saw and knew, they called Him a servant of the devil and wanted to kill Him.

- What did Jesus say in John 15:26 and John 16:8 about the role of the Holy Spirit?

- In Matthew 12:31, Jesus speaks about blasphemy against the Spirit. According to Bible scholar D.A. Carson, to blaspheme the Holy Spirit means seeing "where the truth lies and the light shines" and then **willfully** "turning away from it."[2] What does that mean to you? Had the Pharisees committed blasphemy against the Holy Spirit?

- Finally, according to verse 34, why should we pay attention to the words we speak?

WEEK 4 / DAY 17

MAJOR MOMENT

Jesus said He is the greater Priest, Prophet and King.

We have seen the opposition to Jesus rise throughout Matthew 12. Even after everything they had witnessed Jesus do, many Pharisees refused Jesus, angry that He professed He was both Messiah and God. Then in Matthew 12:38, when they came maliciously asking for "a sign," Jesus made it clear that the "signs" had actually been there all along.

- Matthew 12:39-41 mentions the prophet Jonah. According to Deuteronomy 18:18, what was the job of a prophet?

- In Matthew 12:41, Jesus says, *"and behold, something …"* what?

- Therefore, all prophets were signs pointing to whom?

- Matthew 12:42 mentions Solomon. According to 2 Chronicles 9:22-23, what role did Solomon have and what special attributes?

- In Matthew 12:42, Jesus says, *"and behold, something ..."* what?

- Therefore, all kings and all wisdom were signs pointing to whom?

- Let's jump back a little. Matthew 12:5-6 mentions the priests and the temple. According to Hebrews 5:1, what was the role of the high priest (a serious job that took place within the temple)?

- In Matthew 12:6, Jesus says, *"I tell you, something ..."* what?

- Therefore, all priests, all temple worship and all sacrifices were signs pointing to whom?

See, without Jesus, all of the Old Testament is meaningless. The purpose of the old Jewish ways was to point the world to Jesus Christ. Jesus is the only One who can fulfill it all. Sadly, these Jewish religious leaders were missing this point.

- In Matthew 12:43-45, Jesus used an analogy. The house here represents our lives. In verse 44, the unclean spirit found the house to be what?

- Are we ever content to stop at just having neat and tidy lives? Why or why not? And why is this not enough?

- In Jesus' analogy, the clean but empty life was filled with even more unclean spirits. How do you think we might avoid this happening in our lives?

We can have all the signs in the world and still not see. We can try to be a good person and still be empty. Or we can do something different. We can open our eyes to the signs all around us that are pointing us to Jesus, and we can open the "home" of our heart and invite Him in.

- Jesus says when we do that, He calls us what, according to Matthew 12:50?

- Take a moment to write a prayer thanking Jesus, the greater Priest, Prophet and King, for making you a part of His family.

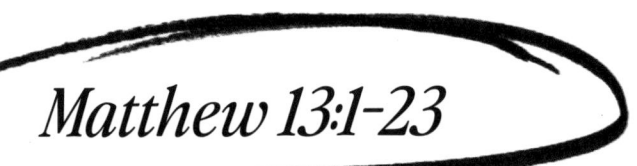

WEEK 4 / DAY 18

Matthew 13:1-23

MAJOR MOMENT
Jesus said there would be varying responses to His message.

So far, we have spent a lot of time looking at the Pharisees and their refusal to believe Jesus. But the Pharisees were not the only ones to struggle. In fact, sometimes today we wonder why some people cannot see or understand what seem to us to be basic spiritual truths. Jesus addressed this very topic in Matthew 13.

- In Matthew 13:3, it says Jesus told them many things in what form?

- The disciples were curious why Jesus did this. What was His answer in verse 11?

- The secrets of the Kingdom are the *mysterion* (Greek for "mysteries") of God. According to 1 Corinthians 2:11, who knows the thoughts of God?

- And the Spirit of Truth will guide us into what, according to John 16:13?

For those of us who have turned to follow Christ, the Spirit of God reveals Truth.
- What happens for the person who has received the understanding that Jesus described, that the disciples had been given? (Matthew 13:11-12)

- And what happens for the person who chooses not to receive this understanding? (v. 12)

Jesus knew some people were going to hear the parables, find them confusing and walk away. Others would lean in, becoming curious, and want to learn more.

- Look back over your walk with Christ. In what ways has the Spirit given you more and more wisdom over time? What might this remind you about God, yourself and others?

Let's jump into Jesus' parable of the sower. In this parable, the sower is Jesus. The seed is the message of salvation. And the soil is the condition of our hearts.

- What is the first soil, mentioned in Matthew 13:4?

- On my family's farm, we have dirt roads going through a few fields to move farm equipment. This dirt is packed down so tightly, the top surface is extremely hard. Imagine throwing seed onto this surface. How does this image help us understand verse 19?

- What is the second soil, mentioned in Matthew 13:5, and what rose to scorch it in verse 6?

- Interesting. The problem for these plants in the rocky soil is that they didn't have the root system to endure the hot sun. How do you think we might develop deeper roots in Christ? (Colossians 2:6-7)

- Plants need sunlight to grow. In Jesus' parable, the sun that means death for the plants growing shallow roots in rocky soil (Matthew 13:21) means life for other plants. (v. 23) In what ways might persecution help us grow in our faith and dependence on God?

- What is the third soil, mentioned in Matthew 13:7?

- Thorns represent the cares of this world. (v. 22) It is interesting to point out that thorns do not immediately choke out a crop. It happens gradually, over time. But once they are established, briars are extremely difficult to get rid of. How does that image certainly describe the cares of this world?

- What is the fourth soil, mentioned in Matthew 13:8?

- Matthew 13:23 says this sowing *"bears fruit."* What might some of this fruit look like? (Galatians 5:22-23)

- How can you pray for the people in your life who might be experiencing tribulation, persecution or "cares of this world" that are challenging their faith today?

Parables of Jesus found in Matthew

Within the pages of Matthew, we see over 20 parables recorded. Parables are stories Jesus used to illustrate a moral or spiritual lesson. Some of the parables have an explanation by Jesus. Others do not. Jesus said He purposefully hid *"the secrets of the kingdom of heaven"* in parables (Matthew 13:11). People would either come to Him for understanding or they would walk away. Truth can be found only in Jesus. When we turn to His words and ask for His guidance to help us understand, we will discover truth that leads us a better way, Jesus' way. And along this path, Jesus says *"blessed are your eyes, for they see, and your ears, for they hear"* (Matthew 13:16).

PARABLE	REFERENCE IN MATTHEW	QUICK MEANING
Salt and Light	5:13-16	Living boldly for Jesus is our mission.
Speck and Log	7:1-5	Judging others is hypocritical.
Wise and Foolish Builders	7:24-27	Build on Jesus for a foundation that lasts.
New Cloth/Old Garment	9:16-17	Old ways make a system for new ways to flourish.
Divided Kingdom	12:24-30	Divided, we fall.
Sower	13:1-23	Heart conditions matter.
Weeds Among Wheat*	13:24-30	Sometimes good and bad look the same at first.
Mustard Seed	13:31-32	God's Kingdom on earth has small beginnings.
Leaven	13:33-34	A little can go a long way in God's Kingdom.

Hidden Treasure*	13:44	Jesus is better than everything.
Pearl of Great Price*	13:45-46	Jesus is worth more than anything.
The Net*	13:47-50	Judgment will come.
Homeowner	13:52	We should know both the Old and the New Testament.
Heart of a Man	15:10-20	Our hearts, attitudes and intentions give our actions meaning.
Lost Sheep	18:10-14	God cares for each and every one of His children.
Unforgiving Servant*	18:23-35	We forgive others because we have been forgiven of much.
Laborers in Vineyard*	20:1-16	Don't despise God's generosity to others.
Two Sons*	21:28-32	Actions speak louder than words.
Tenant Farmers	21:33-45	The way to the Kingdom is to accept the Son.
Marriage Feast	22:1-14	The message of Jesus is for the whole world.
Fig Tree	24:32-35	Jesus is coming soon.
Faithful Servant and Wicked Servant	24:45-51	Be ready for Jesus' return.
Ten Virgins*	25:1-13	Watch and prepare for eternity.
Ten Talents	25:14-30	Don't waste time while you wait for Jesus' return.
Sheep and Goats	25:31-46	Judgment will be eternal for those who are with Jesus and who are not.

(* indicates a parable unique to Matthew and not found in other Gospels)

WEEK 4 / DAY 19

Matthew 13:24-43

MAJOR MOMENT

Jesus said true and false believers will be separated in the end.

Today we move on to another great agricultural parable: the parable of the weeds.
- After reading the parable in Matthew 13:24-30, fill in the chart using verses 36-43.

IMAGE	MEANING
The sower	The Son of Man
The field	
Good seed	
Weeds	
Enemy	
Harvest	
Reapers	

In the Bible Study Fellowship guide to the book of Matthew, I found some interesting historical information. It says, "Jesus' hearers would have been familiar with bearded darnel, a toxic weed that is similar in size and shape to wheat. Enemies sometimes sowed this weed among another farmer's crop to sabotage his harvest. This practice was common enough that Roman law specifically addressed this and required punishment for the crime."[1]

In this parable of the weeds, the devil sneaks in and plants counterfeits. At first, the wheat and weeds look the same.
- What warning does this give us when it comes to spiritual "weeds"? What might weeds look like?

- Read John 8:44. The devil is the father of what?

In Matthew 13:28, the master's servants ask if they should pull out the weeds.
- What does the master say in verse 29?

- It is so hard to tell the wheat from the weeds at the beginning. Plus, focusing on uprooting weeds could uproot wheat unintentionally. What does this remind us of that we also saw in Matthew 7:1 and see in James 4:12?

While we are discouraged from judging the hearts and motives of others, God, who can do so perfectly, certainly will.
- What is the destination for weeds? (Matthew 13:41-42)

- What about the wheat? (v. 43)

- Look back over your notes from this section. What is one practical way you can apply the teaching from these parables to your life today?

Before we close today, let's look at one more verse. Yesterday we talked about how the Spirit reveals Truth to us. It is our choice to lean in and learn or to turn away.

- What do the disciples of Jesus ask Him in Matthew 13:36?

- What are the first two words of verse 37?

- How do those two words bring you peace today?

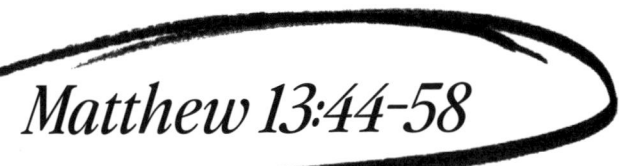

WEEK 4 / DAY 20

Matthew 13:44-58

MAJOR MOMENT

Jesus taught that the Kingdom of heaven is like a great treasure.

Today we are going to take a look at the final four parables of Matthew 13.
- Matthew 13:44 says the kingdom of heaven is like what?

In this time period there were no banks or safety deposit boxes to store items of great value. Therefore, people would often bury treasures to keep them safe. Jesus used an image the people of His day would have been familiar with.
- How does the man respond to finding such a great treasure? (Matthew 13:44)

The second parable is quite similar.
- In Matthew 13:45-46, what does the merchant find, and how does he respond to this find? What does this response teach us about the Kingdom of heaven?

Let's compare this with other scriptures.
- What does Jesus say in Matthew 19:29?

- What does Philippians 3:8 say?

- How would you sum all of this up in one sentence?

- Would you say this is evident in your own life? Why or why not? What has it cost you to follow Christ?

We next find the parable of the net. It has a similar tone as the parable of the weeds, which we studied yesterday.

- What do the men do with the net of fish in Matthew 13:48?

- Like in the parable of the weeds, when will this take place, according to verse 49a?

- The sad reality is that some will reject Jesus. For example, who rejected Jesus in Matthew 13:53-58, and why?

- Sometimes we are tempted to miss the extraordinary because it is wrapped in ordinary skin. How might we guard against this?

  _____
  _____
  _____
  _____

- Verse 58 says Jesus did not do many mighty works in Nazareth because of the people's unbelief. The people refused to see and acknowledge the amazing work Jesus had done, so He didn't do more. What might this teach us?

  _____
  _____
  _____
  _____

Yes, some people will reject the treasure that is Jesus. But others will receive Him with glad and open arms!

- In Matthew 13:52, it says those who pursue the Kingdom are to be like a master of a house, "who _____ _____ of his treasure ..." Does this master cover the treasure? Store it back in a dusty room? What do you think this means?

  _____
  _____
  _____
  _____

We have the new treasure in the New Testament with Jesus, and we have the old treasure in the Old Testament; we have the privilege of seeing how they both come together to form the greatest treasure ever, God's Kingdom.

- In what ways are you sharing your "treasure" (what you are learning about Jesus and the Kingdom of God) with others?

  _____
  _____
  _____
  _____
  _____
  _____
  _____

The world we live in pushes and pulls at our sanity. To live a better way, Jesus' way, we need to understand what the path toward peace looks like. This weekend, let's arrive at our fourth stop.

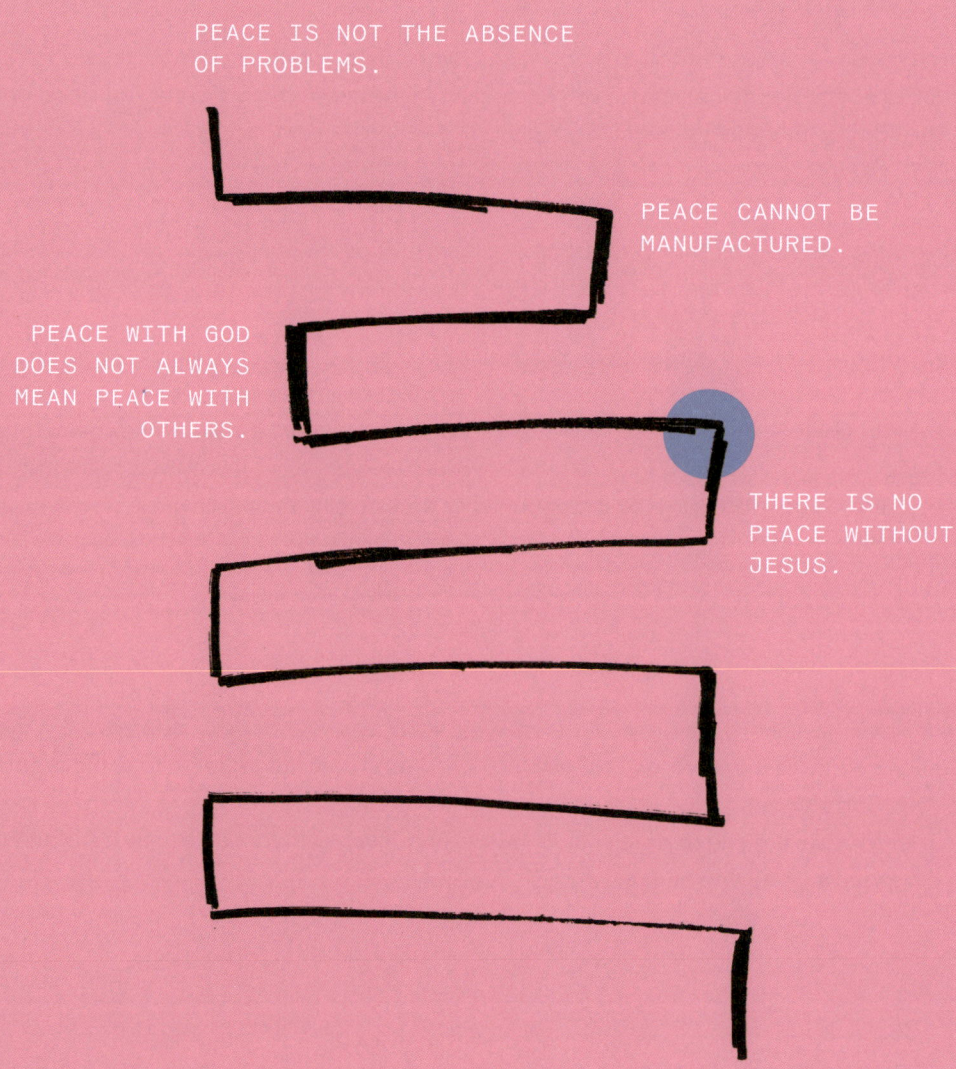

PEACE IS NOT THE ABSENCE OF PROBLEMS.

PEACE CANNOT BE MANUFACTURED.

PEACE WITH GOD DOES NOT ALWAYS MEAN PEACE WITH OTHERS.

THERE IS NO PEACE WITHOUT JESUS.

Weekend Reflection

There is no peace without Jesus.

The world is trying to sell us a counterfeit peace. By the world's standard, we can find peace when we get enough money. Or when we retire. In both cases, doesn't it feel like we must work ourselves to death first?! The world says I'll find peace in vacations or "me time." And while both are nice, and even sometimes necessary, that peace doesn't last. In all of these cases, peace is close to my fingertips but just beyond my grasp. And instead of peace, I find frustration.

In Matthew 13:44-46, Jesus told stories about people who gave up everything to receive a greater treasure. Following Jesus costs us. We don't live like the world. We don't spend like the world. We don't save like the world, rest like the world or retire like the world. Where the world says, "You gotta look out for YOU," Jesus says, "Let it go and look up at Me." This is the only place we will find peace: in Jesus. And if we don't choose Jesus? If we choose to serve ourselves and make our own peace? Jesus said that end looks more like weeping and gnashing of teeth and not like peace at all. (Matthew 13:42; Matthew 13:50)

There is only one path that ends with peace because, friend, **there is no peace without Jesus.** And when the world tells you, "You will have peace when you do X, Y or Z for yourself!" then know it for the lie that it is. If Jesus is not in it, peace will elude you. Rather, peace grows in the soil of Jesus' love and grace. So let's stop buying what the world is selling. Let's see the knockoff for what it is. And let's sell out to the real peace Jesus offers us today.

WEEK
five live

WEEK 5 / DAY 21

Psalm 69

MAJOR MOMENT
God will save His people from the sinking mire.

Today we are going to be switching over to Psalm 69. This is an individual lament psalm "of David," which means it was either written by, about or for King David.

- Read Psalm 69:1-3. When was a time in your life where you felt the way this psalmist felt in these verses? What particular words or phrases stand out to you?

Within Psalm 69, we can see an image of Christ, penned long before Jesus was born in human flesh.

- In Psalm 69:4, the psalmist says there are *"those who hate me _____ _____; mighty are those who would _____ me, those who _____ me with _____."*

- In what ways have we been seeing similar treatment of Jesus through what we have studied in Matthew so far? (For example, see Matthew 12:10-14.)

However, it is also important to point out that, while part of this psalm can be seen as an image of Christ, it was written before Jesus came to earth to show us His better way.

- What did the psalmist pray for in Psalm 69:22-28?

- Yet what did Jesus pray for the people who were hurting Him in Luke 23:34?

Jesus took the sin and shame He truly did not have or deserve, and He bore it for us ...
- According to Psalm 69:19, God knows all of our what? (There are four answers.)

- All of these will cause us affliction and pain, but according to verse 29, God's salvation does what?

- Go back and look at the second word in verse 2, as well as the last three words. Now look again at the phrase for God's salvation in verse 29. What does that mean to you?

Psalm 69:35 says, *"For God will save ..."* Because God willingly sent His Son to bear our sin and shame, we have received deliverance! We ARE saved.
- How does knowing that we ARE eternally saved, right here and now, help in our troubles and hardships?

We can come before the Lord with anything we face, any struggle or hardship or hurt, and we can know He understands. In His humanity, Jesus faced painful circumstances, too.

- What current situation do you need to bring before Jesus today? How can you lay it in His hands?

Psalm 69:13b says God will answer our prayer …

- At a time that is what?

- In the *"abundance"* of what?

- And what kind of faithfulness will He demonstrate?

- In what ways does this verse give you peace?

WEEK 5 / DAY 22

Matthew 14

MAJOR MOMENT

Jesus provided food for the crowds and safety for His disciples.

Matthew 14:3-12 is a historical flashback. Matthew was recalling what had happened to John the Baptist.

- Why was John in prison in the first place? (vv. 3-4)

- What was Jesus' reaction to John's death in verse 13?

- Does this surprise you? Why or why not?

Honestly, if I were Jesus, I think I might have been angry and demanded justice. Yet Jesus quietly withdrew. He knew justice would be served in the end, in God's time. But still, He took a moment. However, the crowds kept following.

- When Jesus saw the great crowd, verse 14 says He had what?

The Greek word used here is *splagchnizomai*. It literally means "to have a deep ache in the stomach."[1] In other words, when Jesus saw the pain and desperation of the crowd, it moved Him to pain, and then to action as He healed the sick.

- What recent news or events have moved you so deeply you "felt them in your gut"? How might you put that feeling of compassion into action?

We next find Jesus' miracle of the feeding of the 5,000. This particular miracle is recorded in all four Gospels.
- Let's record some of the details.

- We just mentioned 5,000 men, but what other details do we see noted by Matthew regarding how many people total were present? (Matthew 14:21)

- Where were they located? What time of day was it? (v. 15) And what resources did they physically have with them? (v. 17)

Sometimes we look at a situation and believe it is too large a task, or maybe it doesn't feel like the right place or the right time to begin something. Maybe we think we don't have enough money, time, talent, brains, etc.
- However, if the task is from God, what would He say about these sentiments?

After this miraculous feeding, Jesus *"immediately"* made the disciples get into a boat (Matthew 14:22). Let's investigate why.

- What does John say in John 6:14-15 about the hearts of the people after this miracle?

___

The disciples did not yet understand Jesus' purpose and mission. They might have agreed with the crowds or at least been easily persuaded by them. In other words, staying on the land with the crowds could have been dangerous to their hearts and minds.

- So instead, Jesus sent them out by boat into the water. According to Matthew 14:24, what was it like out at sea?

___

- Thinking about both the situation on the land and the situation out at sea, what might this teach us about Jesus' definition of "safety"?

___

What felt like a harrowing experience for the disciples ended with them having a chance to witness Jesus' power, both by His walking on water and His calming the wind.

- In Matthew 8, we saw another instance where Jesus calmed the sea. What was the disciples' reaction to this event in Matthew 8:27?

___

- The disciples were starting to learn who Jesus is. What was their reaction to Jesus' miracle we read about today in Matthew 14:33?

___

- Why might surviving life's storms strengthen our faith?

___

WEEK 5 / DAY 23

Matthew 15

MAJOR MOMENT

Jesus taught that it isn't the outside but the heart that matters.

Today we are going to see that what makes a person right with God is a lot less about what we see on the outside, and a lot more about the heart within.

- In Matthew 15:2a, the Pharisees asked Jesus, *"Why do your disciples break the ..."* what?

Within the law of the Old Testament there were certain ritual (or ceremonial) laws concerning washing. These laws were not so much about hygiene as they were about reminding the people that they needed a spiritual cleansing. But over time, scribes began to interpret how they believed God's laws should look in people's lives, and they passed down their interpretations through oral traditions over generations. Such "traditions," added by men over time, are what the Pharisees were referring to in this passage.

- In Matthew 15:3, Jesus answered them by asking, *"And why do you break the ..."* what?

- Just looking at your previous two answers, which do you think is more important?

One of these man-made oral traditions stated that if a person vowed their money and resources to God, but then their aging parents needed to be taken care of, the person would not need to care for their parents because their vow to give to the Lord was more important. However, as Jesus made clear, not caring for (dishonoring) one's parents was a clear violation of God's law.

- There are many books, resources and teachings in the world (even this study guide) that try to help explain Scripture to us. Some are very helpful. However, what is the sole, one and only book we have that has complete authority and Truth? According to 2 Timothy 3:16, where or who does this book come from?

Jesus then addressed the Old Testament ceremonial laws of eating "clean" food. (Matthew 15:10-11) All of this talk about washing and eating was leading up to a very important point …

- What actions or rituals can you think of that look very Christian from the outside? (Note: There is nothing wrong with performing these acts. We are building up to make a point … so go along with us for now …)

- Jesus said that it was not squeaky-clean hands and food that kept a person from being defiled. According to Matthew 15:18, what defiles a person?

- Therefore, all of the Christian actions or rituals you listed above mean nothing if they are not done from a correct heart. What does the correct heart look like?

The disciples' heads would have been spinning at this teaching. As Jews, they had spent their whole lives paying close attention to washing and what they ate. Now Jesus taught that what truly mattered was the heart inside?! This set them up for the next encounter, with a Canaanite woman with great faith.

- Canaanites were considered enemies of the Jewish people. NOT speaking to this woman was exactly what the disciples thought was right. In fact, they even told Jesus to do what? (v. 23)

Jews often referred to gentiles as "dogs," which were wild scavengers. This was a great insult. However, in verse 26 Jesus used the Greek word *kynarion*, or "little dog," which was a more affectionate term, like a household pet. Calling the woman a "dog" would have been common to the disciples' ears; however, using this different variation would have started to pique their attention. And then Jesus commended her faith and answered her request. Her. A Canaanite woman. The disciples' minds would have been blown.

- What mind-blowing teaching do we find in Galatians 3:28? What does that mean for us today?

Matthew 16

WEEK 5 / DAY 24

MAJOR MOMENT

Peter confessed that Jesus was the Christ, the Son of the living God.

Today's reading was a pinnacle in the lives of Jesus' disciples. Their eyes were being opened to the Truth of the Messiah.

To begin, let's look at a couple of people who could not see Christ for who He truly was.
- What two groups of people came to Jesus in Matthew 16:1 and for what reason?

This is interesting. The Pharisees and Sadducees were usually bitterly opposed to one another. And yet here they came together through their shared dislike of Jesus. Jesus knew their intentions and would not give them a sign because He knew they would not truly see it. (v. 4)

Let's think about these two groups. The Pharisees were notoriously self-righteous. The Sadducees, on the other hand, differed from the Pharisees in that they did not believe in a resurrection from the dead. In their minds, this life was all one had, and so they tended to be self-indulgent.
- How do self-righteousness and self-indulgence keep us from truly seeing Jesus? What specific examples can you think of?

The Pharisees and Sadducees were not the only ones who seemed blind to the Messiah.

- In Matthew 16:5-12, Jesus tried to teach His disciples an important spiritual lesson. Yet what thought dominated the disciples' minds? (v. 7)

  _____
  _____
  _____
  _____

- In what ways can a preoccupation with earthly, physical demands also keep us from truly seeing Jesus? What examples can you give?

  _____
  _____
  _____
  _____
  _____
  _____

But the time had come for the disciples' eyes to be opened.

- Jesus asked what people were saying about Him. The disciples replied that people thought Jesus might be John the Baptist, Elijah, Jeremiah, etc. Even today, people have different incorrect opinions on who Jesus is. Some say He was just a prophet. What other explanations have you heard?

  _____
  _____
  _____
  _____
  _____
  _____

- Then Jesus asked the question each and every one of us must answer. He said: *"But who do you say that I am?"* (Matthew 16:15). Write your answer here.

  _____
  _____
  _____
  _____
  _____
  _____

Peter's answer to this question is the foundation of the gospel message.
- What did Peter answer? (v. 16)

_____
_____
_____

For the first time, the disciples truly saw Jesus. They saw Him as the Messiah He was. And now that they could see, it was time for Jesus to show them the plan.
- According to verse 18, Jesus said *"on this rock,"* who *"will build my church"*?

_____
_____
_____

- Hell is where sin, death and Satan reign. According to verse 18, those three things shall not what?

_____
_____
_____

- This is great news! And Jesus wanted His disciples to know exactly HOW this was going to be accomplished. What did Jesus start showing His disciples in verse 21?

_____
_____
_____

In reading this next section, I can't help but think, as we say in the southern United States, "Bless Peter's heart." He went from such a spiritual high to a spiritual low in verses 22-23.
- How does it make you feel hearing about Peter's spiritual ups and downs? Can you relate to Peter in this? Why or why not?

_____
_____
_____
_____

Jesus dying was part of God's ultimate plan for salvation. And Peter wanted to reject that. Satan's oldest trick in the book is to try to convince us that there is a way **around** God's plan. This is why Jesus said to Peter, *"Get behind me, Satan!"* (v. 23a). There is no other plan besides God's plan!

We have seen that self-righteousness, self-indulgence, preoccupation with earthly realities and following our own paths all leave us in the dark, unable to see. Let's look at a better way.

- Matthew 16:24 says we should *"deny [ourselves]."* The *Merriam-Webster Collegiate Dictionary* defines "deny" as "to restrain (oneself) from gratification of desires."[1] What does self-denial look like to you?

- Verse 24 also says to *"take up [our] cross and follow [Him]."* This is a sign of surrender. What does taking up your cross look like to you?

Matthew 17

WEEK 5 / DAY 25

MAJOR MOMENT
Jesus demonstrated His divinity.

In Matthew 16 we saw Peter state the truth of the gospel message: Jesus is the Christ, the Son of the living God. In today's reading we will see Jesus affirm that truth.

- Matthew 17:2 says that Jesus was what?

The Greek word used here is *metamorphothe*, and it is where we get our word "metamorphosis."[1] Jesus went through a complete change. He gave Peter, James and John a glimpse of His divine nature.

- According to John 17:5, what did Jesus have even before the world began?

- And according to Revelation 1:14-15, how will Jesus appear when He comes again?

Peter certainly had his ups and downs. One minute he was making a divine proclamation of Jesus' true identity. The next minute he was trying to tempt Jesus away from the cross. Ouch. Now here at the transfiguration, he made another mistake.

- According to Matthew 17:4, what did Peter want to do?

Moses was the man who gave the Jewish people the Law. Elijah was the voice of the prophets. Both were absolute pillars of the Jewish Old Testament ways.

- Yet WHO does God command Peter and the other disciples to listen to in Matthew 17:5?

- Whose voice should we listen to as well?

- In Matthew 17:8, after the disciples fell down in fear, when they looked up, who alone did they see?

- On who alone should we, too, keep our eyes?

Finally the disciples were beginning to see who Jesus was. Finally He could slowly start to reveal the bigger plan to them. But when they came down the mountain, they found a mess.

- What was the situation in Matthew 17:14-15? And what else was going on in verse 16?

_____
_____
_____
_____
_____
_____

The disciples had been unable to help. What frustration and embarrassment they must have felt. I can imagine the scribes and Pharisees watching in amusement, smirks on their faces. Perhaps the crowd was murmuring, the doubt becoming contagious.

- Read Jesus' reaction in Matthew 17:17. How do you sense He felt?

_____
_____
_____
_____
_____
_____

It seemed everyone was struggling to understand. They had all missed the point, the bigger picture, of what Jesus was all about. They were so focused on the physical, the temporary. Their faith was so fickle that they imagined one "botched miracle" might unravel it all.

- I find this to be convicting. How do you think Jesus feels when He sees us today? How does He find your faith and your focus?

_____
_____
_____
_____
_____
_____

Interestingly, we also find the account of this story in Mark 9:14-29.

- In Mark 9:29, what did Jesus say about this particular demon?

_____
_____
_____
_____

- How's your prayer life, my friend?

In the final account in Matthew 17, we find the incident with the temple tax. The tax was set up to take care of God's house. Jesus used this event, when tax collectors questioned whether He would pay them, to remind Peter of his earlier confession: Jesus is the SON of God.

- Why did Jesus go on to pay the tax, according to verse 27? In what situations might we need to do the same?

This world carries so many worries, and these worries are a threat to our peace. Yet Jesus offers us a better way. This weekend, let's arrive at our fifth stop on the path toward peace.

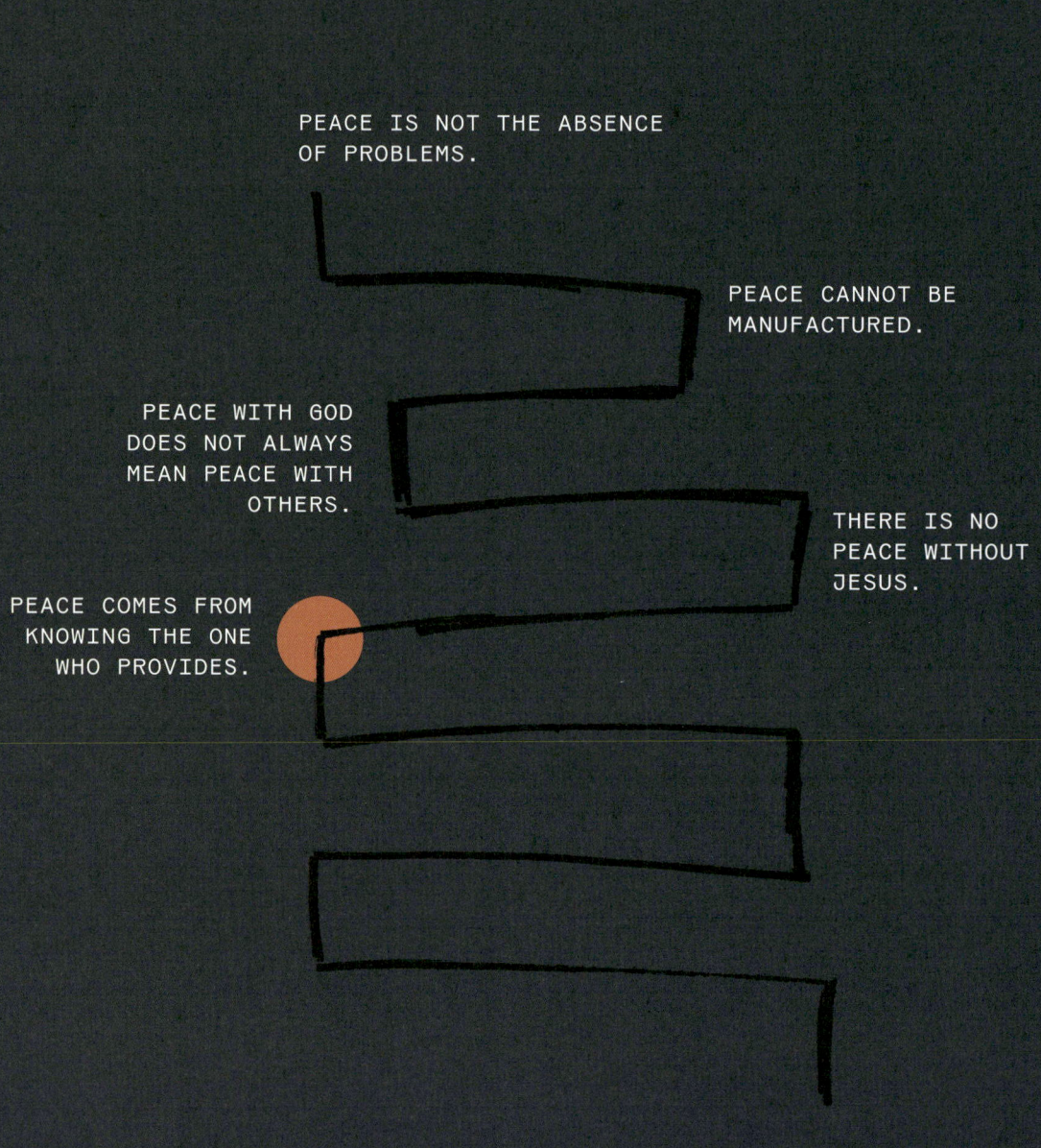

PEACE IS NOT THE ABSENCE OF PROBLEMS.

PEACE CANNOT BE MANUFACTURED.

PEACE WITH GOD DOES NOT ALWAYS MEAN PEACE WITH OTHERS.

THERE IS NO PEACE WITHOUT JESUS.

PEACE COMES FROM KNOWING THE ONE WHO PROVIDES.

Weekend Reflection

Peace comes from knowing the One who provides.

I cannot help but notice all the worry we have seen in the scriptures this week. On numerous occasions the disciples were worried about food. They worried about the storm while they were tossed around in their boat at sea. Then there were the Pharisees, so worried about their sense of power and tradition. There were the crowds, constantly presenting Jesus with their sick loved ones, desperate for a chance at healing. So much worry, fear and anxiety.

And time and time again, Jesus fed. Jesus healed. Jesus taught that there was only One who was truly good. Jesus demonstrated that **He** was the provider of all good things. But His mission was also about so much more than what we need in the here and now. In Matthew 16:26, He said, *"For what will it profit a man if he gains the whole world and forfeits his soul?"* Jesus' mission on earth, first and foremost, was to provide for our souls.

Friends, this is where our peace comes from. **Peace comes from knowing the One who provides.** We can relax and breathe more deeply and calmly because we know Jesus is able to do all things. He can feed crowds from a kid's lunch and walk to us across stormy seas. He can give us purpose and value. He can heal all brokenness. And as followers of Jesus, we know that EVEN IF we do not see it in our lifetime, Jesus will provide absolutely everything He has promised when He returns again. Because our souls have been provided rest in eternity, we can also have peace today.

WEEK 6 / DAY 26

Matthew 18

MAJOR MOMENT

Jesus taught humility, church discipline and forgiveness.

Within Matthew 18, Jesus began to teach His disciples what the Church, His community of followers, would look like and how they should operate.

- To begin, what was the issue the disciples brought up in Matthew 18:1?

- What illustration did Jesus use to describe how His followers should be? (vv. 2-4)

- What childlike qualities do you think Jesus was referring to here (e.g., humility, unconcern for social status, etc.)?

It is important to point out that when Jesus talked about "children" and "little ones" in Matthew 18, He was not just talking about literal children. His bigger reference is to "children of God" – all Christians.

- Therefore, Jesus is telling us to be mindful of our fellow believers: According to verse 6, we should not cause someone else to what? According to verse 7, *"woe to the one by whom"* what comes?

- What does Romans 14:13 say that is similar?

- This is important to remember because, as the parable of the lost sheep demonstrates, what is God the Father's will? (Matthew 18:14)

- As a parent, I can tell you that if someone is unkind to me, that is one thing, but if someone is unkind to my child, the world is about to see a whole new side of me. How might this idea tie into Jesus' teaching about temptation and His parable of the lost sheep?

Unfortunately, no matter how hard we try, issues are going to arise in the Church. And Jesus wanted to lay out principles for handling conflict.

- According to Matthew 18:15, who first gets involved?

- Why might it be so important to start privately in a conflict?

- If this is unsuccessful, what is the next step? (v. 16)

- What reasons can you think of why this might be an important next step?

- What is step three? (v. 17a)

- What is the last resort if none of this works? (v. 17b) And why might this be necessary?

Church discipline is so hard. It is important that it is approached prayerfully and with humble hearts, seeking to win the brother or sister and not just win the argument.
- Jesus gave what assurances regarding church discipline when it is done correctly? (vv. 19-20)

With all this talk about temptation and conflict, it is natural that the next teaching revolves around forgiveness. Take a look at the story Jesus tells in verses 23-35.
- The king's servant who owes 10,000 talents owes a debt equivalent to $6 billion today.[1] Knowing this, why is the servant's statement in verse 26 somewhat ridiculous?

- What remarkable statement do we read in verse 27?

The servant had a fellow servant who owed him a debt of around $12,000 today.[2] For some perspective, this smaller debt is not even 1% of the king's servant's debt. Not even 0.1%. It is 0.0002% of the forgiven 10,000-talent debt. A tiny, tiny fraction. But the servant is unforgiving.
- What does this remind us, both about God's forgiveness toward us and our forgiveness toward others? (vv. 33-35)

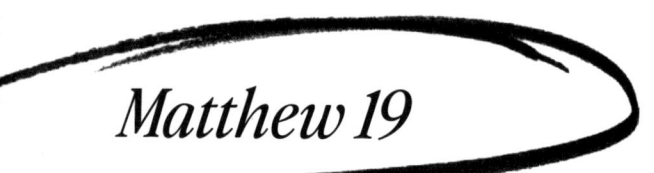

Matthew 19

WEEK 6 / DAY 27

MAJOR MOMENT
Jesus' teachings were often countercultural.

So much of today's study is going to involve looking at the historical context of the time to help us understand what exactly was being said.

Let's start with divorce. There were two camps of thought during this time period. One side believed a man could divorce his wife for almost any reason. (For example, if she "spoiled a dish for him" or "if he found another fairer than she."[1]) In the other camp, the idea was that a man could only divorce his wife if she was unfaithful to him. Notice, during this time period, only a man could initiate divorce, and the focus was only on **his wife's** unfaithfulness.

The Pharisees asked Jesus a question about divorce in Matthew 19:3 to *"test him"* to see how He would interpret the law. But Jesus cut right to the heart.

- Jesus reminded them that, from the beginning, God created who to be equal? (v. 4) And at marriage, the two shall become what? (v. 5)

_____

_____

_____

_____

Essentially Jesus was saying something very countercultural. He was stating that women are not property, and marriage is not a transaction. Marriage is sacred. It is not to be taken lightly.

- Looking at our culture today, what do you think is society's attitude regarding marriage? Why?

_____

_____

_____

_____

_____

_____

Jesus was so serious and strong on His teachings about marriage that the disciples actually wondered if it was worth being married! (v. 10) Jesus did not necessarily disagree with them. For some, singleness is a worthy way of life. (v. 12) I like how the Bible Study Fellowship book on Matthew puts it: "We are to support unmarried people, not pity, pressure, or treat them as though God has withheld His best from them."[2]

- What single people do you know? How can you love, support and welcome them today? If you are a single person, how would you like to see the Church support you?

_____
_____
_____
_____
_____

Another group of people who were often dismissed in ancient Jewish culture was children, particularly young children who could not yet work. Jesus welcomed them with open arms. (vv. 14-15)

- What groups of people are sometimes dismissed or forgotten in our society today? What is one thing you could do to honor them this week?

_____
_____
_____
_____
_____

Finally, we reach the story of the young rich man. Pay special attention to what the young man asked.

- In Matthew 19:16 he said, *"Teacher, what _____ _____ must I do to have eternal life?"*

If you're not sure what to think about this question, allow me to illustrate in a different context. Mike Powell holds the world record for long jump at 8.95 meters (or a little over 29 feet). Astonishing! To give you something to compare that to, I tested my own abilities and sadly jumped only 5 feet. (Don't laugh!) So it is true Mike Powell is a better jumper than I am. However, what if you put Mr. Powell and me at the edge of the Grand Canyon and told us to jump to the other side? At one point, the width of the canyon is around 18 miles (or over 95,000 feet). Would the world record holder jump farther than me? Absolutely. Would it matter? Not a bit.

- What does this remind us about our "good deeds" (like our long-jump abilities) gaining us eternal life (like crossing the canyon-esque divide between sinners and a holy God)?

Jews during this time period believed the rich had found favor with God. The wealthy were extra blessed, and so surely they were first in line to receive salvation from God. This is why Jesus' statements astonished His disciples in Matthew 19:21-30. They had believed that obedience to God led to earthly rewards, and disobedience would lead to punishment. Jesus teaches that this doesn't look exactly as they first thought. The true reward of obedience is better.

- According to verse 28, when will followers of Jesus see a reward? And according to verse 29, that reward will be to inherit what?

Matthew 20

WEEK 6 / DAY 28

MAJOR MOMENT
Jesus taught and demonstrated that the first will be last and that greatness is found in serving.

We left off in Matthew 19:30 with Jesus' statement that *"many who are first will be last, and the last first."* In Chapter 20, Jesus then used the parable of the laborers in the vineyard to illustrate this point. It is important to point out that the *"denarius"* or payment in this parable does not represent working for salvation (as we cannot work for our salvation; see Ephesians 2:8-9). No, this parable is all about **attitude** in light of God's generosity.

- To give the proper context, go back up to Matthew 19:27. What question did Peter ask Jesus?

This is the heart issue addressed in this parable. Sometimes we start to think in terms of what we will **get** from God because of the work we have done. We operate like the first workers, who arbitrate a deal with the master. They want to know exactly what they are going to receive before they go out to work. (Matthew 20:2)

- Notice the following hired workers. According to Matthew 20:4, what amount of payment do the rest agree to work for?

- Right from the start, what attitude differences can you see between the first group and the following?

Friends, here is the truth: God owes us nothing. Read that again. *He owes us nothing.* And as it says in verse 15, God has the right to give and take as He pleases. He is perfect and holy. Which means the very fact that God would call us to Him and give us salvation, and then allow us opportunities to serve Him, is **miraculous**! That is generosity above and beyond what any of us deserve. This is why the attitude of the first servants both starts and ends in a bad place.

- Do you ever find yourself identifying with the first workers? Why or why not? What reminders do we need to protect our hearts from the same attitude problem they have?

In Matthew 20:17-19, Jesus predicted, for the third time, His death. Except this time, He told His disciples exactly how He would die, and He reiterated that He would resurrect on the third day.

- The purpose and focus of His life on earth was always on the forefront of His mind. According to verse 28, what two things did Jesus mention He came to do?

- The disciples still did not understand, as we see in the account that follows. James and John wanted thrones. (Matthew 20:20-23) Why might they have asked for this? (See Matthew 19:28.)

The disciples heard Jesus' words and did what we all tend to do so often: They interpreted them selfishly. They looked for how His words could benefit them.

- Do you ever notice selfish tendencies in your own heart? List an example or two.

- Notice: After James and John (and their dear momma) made this request, did Jesus get mad?

- Did Jesus grant their request?

- We can bring all of our requests to God, even the selfish ones. He listens and loves us. And He will answer as He sees fit and always do what is best for us. How does knowing that bring you peace today?

- According to Matthew 20:26-28, what does true greatness look like?

Jesus demonstrated that very thing when, on His way to Jerusalem, toward pain, suffering and death, He stopped. He turned, saw and listened to two blind men, and healed them. (Matthew 20:29-34)
- How can you stop, turn, look and listen to someone around you today, even if you are walking your own road of hardship and pain?

WEEK 6 / DAY 29

Matthew 21:1-22

MAJOR MOMENT
Jesus began His final week by boldly entering Jerusalem and the temple.

Yesterday we looked at how Jesus did many wonderful things on earth, but His main focus was always on the cross. Perhaps to emphasize this, Matthew spends eight chapters detailing Christ's final week here on earth. Today, we jump into this account, starting with the triumphal entry into Jerusalem.

- To begin, read the messianic prophecy found in Zechariah 9:9. What did this say would happen during the time of the Messiah?

_____
_____
_____
_____

These crowds had been following Jesus. These crowds knew the prophetic words. And now they were seeing Jesus fulfill them. He HAD to be the Messiah! What a moment!

- What do they cry out in Matthew 21:9?

_____
_____
_____
_____

- This comes specifically from Psalm 118:26. Look closely at the verse before it: Psalm 118:25. What specifically did they believe was about to happen?

_____
_____
_____
_____

I often marvel at these crowds. So passionate about calling Jesus the Messiah on Palm Sunday. So passionate about crying out "Crucify Him!" on the following Friday. What happened? There are many answers, but one of the biggest factors was their shortsightedness. They truly believed on Sunday that Jesus was about to deliver them from Rome. That's all they wanted. Relief in the here and now. A fix for their generation. And when they began to see that Jesus would not be providing this, they no longer wanted Him.

- What times can you think of when you wanted immediate relief, answers or help more than you wanted Jesus? How does it bring some comfort and peace to know that His plan, though we don't always see or understand it, is always bigger and better?

This particular day marked the beginning of the Passover week commemorating God's deliverance of Israel from Egypt. (Exodus 12) So many people were in Jerusalem, often from different regions or countries. They had to exchange currency. Then they needed to purchase the animals for sacrifice. Merchants saw an opportunity to make big money by inflating the prices and exchange rates.

- How did Jesus feel about this? (Matthew 21:12-13)

- What do you notice about the people or events that anger Jesus?

- It was common knowledge that those who were blind and lame could not enter the temple. (Leviticus 21:18) Yet, in verse 14, the blind and the lame came in, and Jesus healed them. What does this teach us about Jesus?

In Matthew 21:18-22, we have an acted-out parable that perhaps also clarifies why Jesus did what He did at the temple in Jerusalem. These events unfolded sometime during the month of April, when fig trees would have been filled with green leaves, and edible buds would have been forming. So this particular green tree looked alive, healthy and beautiful. But it had no fruit. Sort of like a temple filled with hollow sacrifices. Or religion without substance.

- How might this apply to our own lives as well?

_____
_____
_____
_____
_____
_____
_____

In verses 21-22, Jesus commanded His disciples to pray, *"and whatever you ask in prayer, you will receive, if you have faith."* Now, this is not a blank check so believers can fill in whatever they choose and it will be granted them. God is not a genie in a lamp, granting whatever we wish. Rather, this is Jesus saying we need to pray **big, bold** prayers! We need to pray for the impossible, like for mountains to be thrown into the sea. Why? Because we serve a God who can **do the impossible.**

- How would you describe your prayers? Are they big and bold? Why or why not? What impossible thing do you need to bring to God in faith today?

_____
_____
_____
_____
_____
_____
_____

Holy Week Timeline

(As seen in Matthew)

SUNDAY

Jesus' Triumphal Entry Into Jerusalem (21:1-11)

MONDAY

Jesus Cleared the Temple (21:12-13)
Jesus Cursed Fig Tree (21:18-19)

TUESDAY

Jesus Taught Lesson of the Fig Tree (21:20-22)

Jesus Questioned by Religious Leaders (21:23-23:39)

Jesus Gave "Olivet Discourse" (24:1-25:46)

WEDNESDAY

Religious Leaders Plotted To Kill Jesus (26:3-5)

Disciples Prepared for Passover (26:17-19)

THURSDAY

Passover/Last Supper (26:20-35)

Jesus Prayed in Gethsemane (26:36-46)

~ Around midnight ~

Jesus Betrayed by Judas and Arrested (26:47-56)

FRIDAY

Jewish trials (26:57-27:2)

Roman trials (27:2-26)

~ Around 9 a.m.-3 p.m. ~

Crucifixion (27:27-54)

~ Around evening time ~

Burial (27:57-61)

SATURDAY

Silence

SUNDAY

Empty Tomb (28:1-8)
Resurrection Witnesses (28:9-20)

WEEK 6 / DAY 30

Matthew 21:23-46

MAJOR MOMENT
Jesus knew the hearts and plans of the religious leaders.

As we continue to travel with Jesus through what we often refer to as "Holy Week," leading up to His crucifixion, we see that the events of today's reading took place on Tuesday. After driving out the merchants and welcoming the sick and disabled into the temple the day before, when Jesus returned, the religious leaders were waiting for Him.

- What question did they ask Jesus in Matthew 21:23?

If Jesus said His authority to teach and heal came from God, He would be claiming to be the Messiah. According to Old Testament law, claiming to BE God as a human was blasphemous, and they could arrest and kill Him. If Jesus said His authority came from man, then He was a "nobody," and the crowds would have been disappointed. But Jesus knew the religious leaders' trick and played it back on them. He asked them about John the Baptist's authority.

- The leaders knew that if they answered that John the Baptist's came from heaven, then how would they be trapped? (v. 25)

- But if they said it was from man, who would disapprove of them? (v. 26)

- Notice the leaders' thoughts. They were not interested in discovering the truth. What, perhaps, were they more interested in?

- There are many answers to the above question, but one that comes to my mind is that the leaders desperately wanted to win their argument. How can we make sure we are after **TRUTH** and not "winning" in our discussions with people around us?

To further reveal their hearts and plans, Jesus offered two parables.
- Who do you think the two sons represent in the parable in Matthew 21:28-32?

- How dangerous it is to say we follow Jesus but not follow through in our hearts! How does this tie back to the acted-out parable of the fig tree in Matthew 21:18-19?

- In the parable of the tenants in Matthew 21:33-44, what happened to the first servants who were sent to the people?

- These first servants represent the prophets. Read 2 Chronicles 24:20-21, Jeremiah 26:8 and Matthew 14:10. How did the people treat the prophets?

- Jesus, in this parable of the tenants, is the son. By telling this parable, what did Jesus show He knew about the actual plans of the religious leaders? (Matthew 21:38-39)

Jesus then quoted Psalm 118:22 and talked about the cornerstone.
- According to Acts 4:11, who is the cornerstone?

Some people would find the cornerstone, and from there, they would build up the Church. Others would stumble over it, not able to accept it. And ultimately, in the end, the cornerstone will crush in judgment anyone who has not accepted it. But the key to all of this is **the cornerstone.**
- Read the next verse, Acts 4:12. What does this say?

Instead of repenting, the religious leaders in Matthew 21 only became angrier. Jesus had read and revealed their hearts, and it wasn't pretty. Take a moment today to ask God to reveal your own heart. Pray for a soft heart of repentance toward the loving correction of the Father.

It is not easy to have peace in a world full of fallible humans. To live a better way, Jesus' way, we need to look to His guidelines when it comes to relating with others. Surprisingly, the path looks a lot like first knowing ourselves. This weekend, let's arrive at our sixth stop.

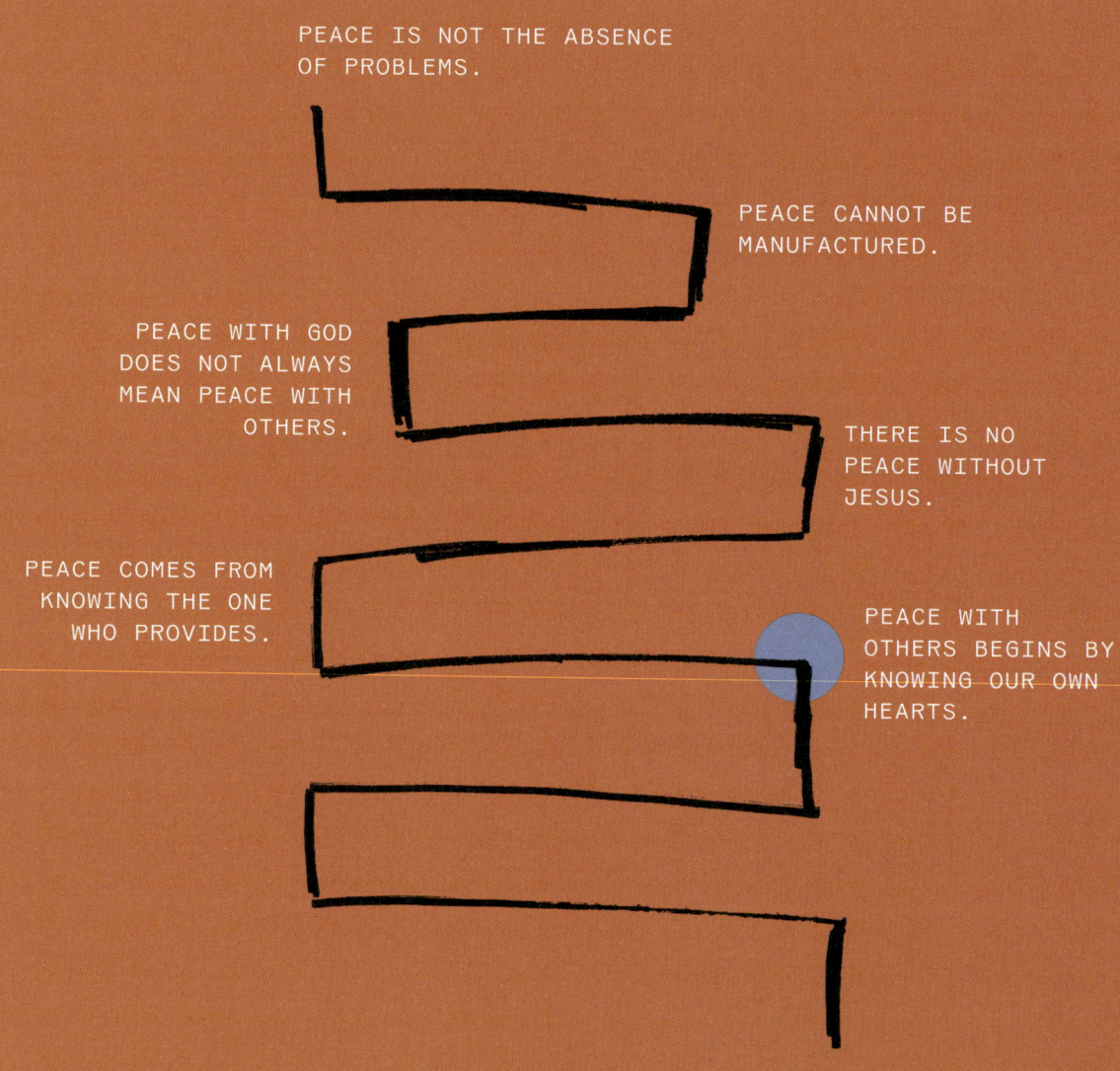

PEACE IS NOT THE ABSENCE OF PROBLEMS.

PEACE CANNOT BE MANUFACTURED.

PEACE WITH GOD DOES NOT ALWAYS MEAN PEACE WITH OTHERS.

THERE IS NO PEACE WITHOUT JESUS.

PEACE COMES FROM KNOWING THE ONE WHO PROVIDES.

PEACE WITH OTHERS BEGINS BY KNOWING OUR OWN HEARTS.

Weekend Reflection

Peace with others begins by knowing our own hearts.

In our reading this week, Jesus dealt with misguided disciples; He talked about church discipline and forgiveness, and He even dealt with angry religious leaders. On their own, the disciples squabbled about who was greatest, and the leaders attempted to find reasons to arrest and kill Jesus. There certainly did not seem to be peace amongst the people. So what would Jesus say was the key to peace in all of this?

Jesus knew having peace with others would not be easy. And sometimes, it wasn't completely possible (i.e. between Him and the religious leaders). But Jesus did teach us an important principle: **Peace with others begins by knowing our own hearts.** It is easier to forgive our brother or sister when we are reminded of our own insurmountable debt, which the Father has forgiven for us. (Matthew 18:23-35) Peace will happen naturally when we remember our "greatness" comes from humility and serving and being last. (Matthew 18:4; Matthew 20:26-28) It will help us get along with others when we stop comparing ourselves to each other. We need to know, deep in our souls, that even though our hearts pull us toward those things of temporary wealth and relief, Jesus sees the bigger picture of eternity. Our greatest reward is not in the here and now but in the new world to come! Our reward is eternal, perfect life with Him. (Matthew 19:23-29) When we **know** we have that, all comparison fades.

Peace with others is not easy. But it can be easier when we follow Jesus' ways. And peace starts by taking a good, long look at our own hearts and reminding ourselves what really matters. When our own hearts are at peace, peace with others can begin.

WEEK seven

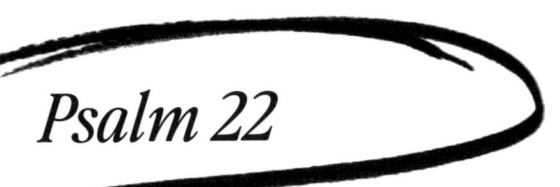

WEEK 7 / DAY 31

MAJOR MOMENT

God is present and faithful, even when His people experience great suffering.

Psalm 22 speaks to much of what we will see in these last two weeks of our Matthew study.
- To begin, read Psalm 22 in its entirety. Ask the Holy Spirit to guide your reading and bring to life particular words or phrases that He might have you see today. Jot those down here, along with your thoughts.

While the greater fulfillment of this passage is the crucifixion of Jesus, it is important to remember that it first was an individual cry of lament. I found myself remembering times in my life where I vividly felt anguish like the author, David, as well. One of the (many) things I love about Psalm 22 is that it teaches us what it can look like to walk through suffering. Let's break down the sections of this psalm.
- In Psalm 22:1-2, how does the writer feel about God?

- Verse 3 begins with the words "*Yet you ...*" What does the writer remind himself about God in Psalm 22:3-5?

- The pendulum swings back the other way in verses 6-8. What comes to the writer's mind?

- Verse 9 begins with the words "*Yet you ...*" This time the reminder is even more personal. Who specifically is God caring for in verses 9-11? (Hint: *"Yet you are he who took ____ from the womb; you made ____ trust you at my mother's breasts."* [v. 9])

- The attention switches again in verses 12-18. What three animals are used to portray the enemy? What do these have in common?

- And then verse 19 begins with the words "*But you, O LORD...*" How I love these words! Notice most of the lines in verses 19-21 are written **as present-tense cries to God, asking Him to** *"come quickly ... deliver my soul ... save me."* What is different about verse 21b?

- The psalm ends in verses 22-31 with praise. Underline every time you see the words *praise, glorify* or *worship*. (I found seven.)

Let's take a moment to look at this structure we just outlined. The first thing that stands out: It is OK to have struggles or doubts or to cry out honestly to God ... even to yell out at Him, "Where are You?!" And if you have ever felt this way, you are **not alone.** David and, as we will soon see, Jesus Himself felt and cried out the same in their seasons of immense suffering. It is OK to come honest and raw before God.

- How does knowing this bring you some peace in the hard times?

- However, also notice how the psalmist kept interrupting his thoughts and bringing them back to God's faithful goodness. Why is it so important that we interrupt our thinking sometimes? I particularly like the phrase "preaching to my own heart." What does that mean to you?

- And finally, we see the importance of praise. Look up Psalm 147:1. What does this say about praise? The ESV Bible titles Psalm 147 *"He Heals the Brokenhearted."*[1] Why does that seem fitting, especially after today's psalm study?

To end today, we are going to highlight some important, prophetic verses from Psalm 22 that will be good to keep in our minds, especially coming up in Week 8. For each verse, simply write down what it says so it is fresh in your mind.

PSALM 22:1	
PSALM 22:7	
PSALM 22:8	
PSALM 22:18	

WEEK 7 / DAY 32

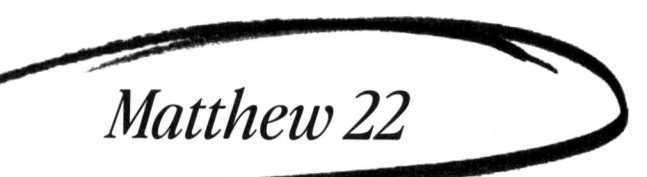
Matthew 22

MAJOR MOMENT

Religious leaders attempted to trap Jesus with words.

Matthew 22 starts with a parable with a similar meaning to ones we studied in Matthew 21 (the parable of the two sons and the parable of the wicked tenants.) But there is one particular difference we want to look at today.

- What happens in Matthew 22:11-13?

- Read Isaiah 61:10. Where alone can our clean "wedding garments" come from?

The rest of Matthew 22 has the religious leaders attempting to trap Jesus with their words. This would be a way they could get rid of Him without having to dirty their own hands. Plus, I'm guessing they thought they could easily outwit some carpenter from Nazareth ...

MATTHEW 22:15-22 - PHARISEES AND HERODIANS ASKED A POLITICALLY CHARGED QUESTION. The Pharisees were known for being anti-Rome. The Roman taxes were oppressive to the Jewish people. Plus, the Romans were pagans. The Herodians were known to be pro-Rome. They supported the "Herods" being in power and often worked with the Roman occupation. Their question about taxes was a trick because if Jesus agreed with the tax, He would infuriate the people. If He did not agree with the tax, the Herodians could accuse him of insurrection to Rome.

- What was Jesus' reply in verses 20-21?

Taxes and civil codes may belong to the government, but our souls and eternity belong to God. Human governments, even the very best we have, no matter the leader, ALL are flawed. And while governments are due a certain level of respect (and, yes, taxes), no government or political affiliation has naming rights to our souls. Our eternity rests securely in the hands of God.

- How does knowing this bring you peace today?

___

MATTHEW 22:23-33 - SADDUCEES ASKED A THEOLOGICALLY CHARGED QUESTION.
The Sadducees were a people group who believed primarily in the Pentateuch (aka the first five books of the Old Testament, Genesis through Deuteronomy). They believed there was no mention of resurrection in these books, and therefore, resurrection was impossible. They asked Jesus a question about marriage and resurrection to show why they believed resurrection was absurd.

- What did Jesus say in Matthew 22:29?

___

Jesus was clear that even the Pentateuch teaches the idea of resurrection. God is God of the living! (v. 32) Jesus also said they did not understand the *"power of God"* (v. 29). Eternity will not be just some extension of life on earth as we know it. (v. 30) And while we don't know all the details, we can trust in the power of God to make every relationship we have in eternity deeper and better than we could ever imagine.

- How does knowing this bring you peace today?

___

MATTHEW 22:34-40 - AN EXPERT IN THE LAW ASKED A CLARIFYING QUESTION.
Jesus had been stumping the Pharisees, the Herodians and the Sadducees right and left. Witnessing this tremendous authority, one religious law expert piped up with the question of questions. See, there was a question that religious leaders loved to debate during this time period. The Jewish people at this time had a documented 613 commandments in the law: 248 commands about what to do and 365 about what not to do.[1] Because it would be so difficult to fully obey all the commands, experts

tried to define which of the commandments were "heavy" (important) and which were "light" (less important). That way a person could especially focus on the heavy commandments. This was a source of constant debate for leaders.

- How did Jesus answer in Matthew 22:37-39?

    _____
    _____
    _____
    _____

- Take a look at the image below. In the middle is you. There is a big arrow pointing up to God. The smaller arrows from the sides are pointing toward other people. Use verses 37-39 to label these arrows "My first love" and "My second love."

It is important to remember that love for others is made possible by our first love, God. You might think of it like a fountain. As our love for God goes up, that love naturally overflows onto others.

- What does this image remind you about loving both God and others?

MATTHEW 22:41-46 - JESUS ASKED A QUESTION TO THE RELIGIOUS LEADERS.
Now it was Jesus' turn to ask them a question. And an important question it is. See, the religious leaders believed the coming Messiah would be a son of David … a man … who came to establish an earthly kingdom. Jesus was that son. However, Jesus showed them that even David knew the Messiah was more than just a man. The Messiah would be Lord. God.

Friends, it is the same question every single one of us must answer sooner or later as well: Is Jesus just some good man who once lived, or is He God, and Lord of my life?

- What is your answer to that question today?

- Does this answer bring you peace? Why or why not? (If not, we would love to continue the conversation with you about how a life surrendered to Jesus as Lord is a life of great joy and peace. You can visit us online at @proverbs31ministries, or start up a conversation with other Bible readers in our First 5 app.)

WEEK 7 / DAY 33

Matthew 23

MAJOR MOMENT

Jesus denounced the religious leaders.

In Chapter 22, we witnessed a bit of a showdown between Jesus and the religious leaders. In today's chapter, Jesus did not mince words when He got straight to the heart of the problem. We have studied much of Matthew together, and yet rarely have we seen such strong, almost angry, words from Jesus. Notice these scathing words were not for the obviously lost or obviously sinful. No, these words were directed to the "religious." Oh, what a warning to us as well. Let's take a look at these denouncements and examine our own hearts today.

- Read the last sentence of Matthew 23:3 and the first sentence of verse 5. Why do you think we try to sound or look "better" than we are?

_____
_____
_____
_____
_____
_____

Jesus then issued seven woes to these religious elite. Let's break them down.

VERSE 13 - WOE TO THOSE WHO SHUT THE DOOR.

- The religious were making God seem impossible to reach and please, essentially shutting the door to God in the faces of lost people looking for Him. In what ways might the same be happening today?

_____
_____
_____
_____
_____

VERSE 15 - WOE TO THOSE WHO MAKE CONVERTS WORSE THAN THEMSELVES.
- Converts tend to look like the ones who converted them. This meant that legalistic leaders made even-more-legalistic followers. Why is it so important that we are always monitoring our hearts, both as mentors and mentees? (And we are all both!)

VERSES 16-22 - WOE TO BLIND GUIDES.
- During this time, Pharisees would weigh oaths, deciding which were more important to keep. They were looking for loopholes, twisting the details and basically missing the point: Loving God and others is most important. What is one way we can remind ourselves today that God comes first?

VERSES 23-24 - WOE TO THOSE WHO TRADE WHAT'S IMPORTANT FOR WHAT'S NOT.
- In Old Testament law, a gnat was considered unclean. The Pharisees were so concerned about being ceremonially clean that they would strain their water so they would not even accidentally swallow a gnat. But a camel, the largest animal known in the Middle East during this time, was also an unclean animal. What are some "gnat" issues that have your focus today? What bigger ("camel") issues can you focus on instead? (See verse 23 for examples.)

VERSES 25-26 - WOE TO THOSE WHO ARE CLEAN OUTSIDE BUT NOT INSIDE.
- Our outside righteous deeds mean very little if they are not the reflection of our inside relationship with Jesus. What does that statement mean to you?

VERSES 27-28 - WOE TO THOSE WHO LOOK BEAUTIFUL BUT ARE DEAD INSIDE.
- Only Jesus knows our hearts. What does this remind you about yourself and others?

VERSES 29-32 - WOE TO THOSE WHO SAY, "WELL, I WOULD NEVER DO THAT."
- The Pharisees liked to say they never would have been like their ancestors and never would have killed the prophets. Yet Jesus knew they were about to have Him killed. Why might it be dangerous for us to develop a mentality of "Well, I would never do that"?

I found Matthew 23 to be convicting. What a challenge to my own heart to examine my motives and mindset! This is why I love how Jesus ends this chapter ...
- Read Matthew 23:37. How would you describe Jesus' heart here?

- Jesus longs to restore us — but only if we are willing. Take a moment to pray, telling Jesus you are willing to walk the road of restoration and holiness.

WEEK 7 / DAY 34

Matthew 24

MAJOR MOMENT
Jesus prophesied the end.

It is interesting how there is a natural human fascination about the end of time. We have movies and books that suggest different scenarios of how the world or humanity ends. We can even read news sources or science reports that offer scary predictions.

- What are a few of the ways people have envisioned the end of the world as we know it?

- How do these ideas make you feel?

It is as though we instinctively know that the world and humankind are headed to some kind of endpoint. And we aren't wrong! The Bible teaches the same.

- Read Revelation 21:1-3. What point in the future is all creation headed toward?

In Matthew 24, the disciples also had questions about the end of time. And Jesus was not shy about answering their curiosity. Similar to the stylings of the Old Testament prophets, Jesus gave His prophecy of the end of time but did so by speaking of both near and far-off events simultaneously, and not necessarily in chronological order. On one hand, Jesus referred to the end of ancient Judaism (as it was practiced in the temple) by predicting the destruction of the temple by Rome in A.D. 70. Yet Jesus was also referring to the end times to come, a time when Jesus will return and judge the world for eternity.

Let's look at some of the things we can take away from this passage.

- Matthew 24:22b says *"But for the sake of the elect ..."* what will happen?

  _____
  _____
  _____

- Jesus told of great suffering and hardship and yet sent this reminder that, even if it looks like all catastrophe and bad news, **God is still in control.** Copy this sentence: *No matter what, God is in control.*

  _____
  _____

- Matthew 24:29 gives what scary-sounding signs?

  _____
  _____
  _____

- In verse 29, the sky is literally falling. But in Matthew 24:30-31, who appears and why?

  _____
  _____
  _____
  _____

- Copy this sentence: *No matter what, do not lose hope. Jesus is coming.*

  _____
  _____

- Look over these last few responses. How do these truths make you feel, and how does that compare to the world's end times suggestions you mentioned at the beginning of today? Describe why Jesus' way can bring us peace.

  _____
  _____
  _____
  _____
  _____
  _____

Jesus then gave another lesson of a fig tree (a little different from the one we studied on Day 29). People could watch this tree and see summer was near. But they could not hurry up the blooming of the fig tree or the coming of summer. They simply watched, waited and anticipated its coming.

- What does the fig tree lesson remind us about the end times?

- What does Matthew 24:36 remind us? Why might it be a good thing that we do not know?

Maybe after reading Matthew 24, you feel like you have more questions than answers. "Are we in the end times?! Are these the signs?!" we might ask. But let's leave here with one last thought. **Matthew 24 is not about calculation. It is about preparation.** There is really only one question that matters.

- Are you prepared for the end times? How can we all better prepare our hearts to see Jesus?

Matthew 25

WEEK 7 / DAY 35

MAJOR MOMENT
Jesus illustrated how to be ready for His return.

Yesterday we looked at Jesus' prophecies regarding the end times. Today we are looking at the second part of this teaching, where Jesus used three illustrations to explain to us how to be ready for His return. These illustrations have some elements in common: Each mentions two different groups or types of people, and each contains a moment where the people are surprised. The best way to look at a parable is to take a step back to find the major point. Let's do that for the three illustrations in Matthew 25.

MATTHEW 25:1-13 - THE PARABLE OF THE 10 VIRGINS

- Who are the two different groups or types of people in this parable? (v. 2)

- What is their moment of surprise? (vv. 6, 12)

- Taking a step back, what is the main point of this parable? (Jesus helps us with this in verse 13.)

- In the story, each virgin is individually responsible for her own lamp. In the end, we cannot rely on someone else (besides Jesus) for our salvation. What does that mean to you?

The parable of the 10 virgins reminds us to prepare, wait and watch for Jesus' return. But that doesn't mean we sit around and twiddle our thumbs. It doesn't mean we do nothing! Let's look at the next parable.

MATTHEW 25:14-30 - THE PARABLE OF THE TALENTS
- Who are the different types of people in this parable? (vv. 15-18)

- What is their moment of surprise? (v. 19)

- Taking a step back, what is the main point of this parable?

- It is interesting that the man with one talent didn't spend it on some self-indulgence or gamble it away. He simply did nothing. (vv. 25-29) What does that mean to you?

- Notice in verses 24-25, who does the man blame for his inaction? In what ways do people do the same today?

It is our privilege and responsibility to use every second of life God has gifted us to bring glory and honor to Him. Because, sooner or later, judgment is coming.

MATTHEW 25:31-46 - THE PARABLE OF THE SHEEP AND THE GOATS (FINAL JUDGMENT)
- Who are the two different types of people in this parable? (vv. 32-33)

- What is their moment of surprise? (vv. 37-40, 44-45)

- Taking a step back, what is the main point of this parable?

- Let's point out that the sheep's "righteous deeds" alone are not what allow them into the eternal Kingdom. What does Ephesians 2:8-9 remind us?

- This parable confirms the fact that, while sometimes good deeds might appear from an unredeemed heart, a redeemed heart will **absolutely** start to walk toward righteous deeds. They are the natural overflow of a life filled with Jesus. And if we say we love Jesus, but we do not have a heart of compassion and love expressing itself through our actions, we need to ask ourselves if our relationship with Jesus is true. In what ways have you seen your own walk with Jesus result in increasing good deeds?

Jesus reminded His people to watch, prepare and wait for His return. While we wait, we do everything we can to glorify Him, using the resources, talents and abilities He has given us. Because one day soon, judgment will be here. And we don't have to be surprised by it. We can be excited and ready because eternity will be ours in Him.

- How does this bring you peace today?

It is not easy to have peace in a world full of problems. We can focus on the problems, or we can put our focus on our Savior. Rest assured — Jesus' path toward peace is the better way. This weekend, let's arrive at our seventh stop.

PEACE IS NOT THE ABSENCE OF PROBLEMS.

PEACE CANNOT BE MANUFACTURED.

PEACE WITH GOD DOES NOT ALWAYS MEAN PEACE WITH OTHERS.

THERE IS NO PEACE WITHOUT JESUS.

PEACE COMES FROM KNOWING THE ONE WHO PROVIDES.

PEACE WITH OTHERS BEGINS BY KNOWING OUR OWN HEARTS.

PEACE IS KEEPING OUR EYES ON ETERNITY WITH JESUS.

Weekend Reflection

Peace is keeping our eyes on eternity with Jesus.

In our reading this week, Jesus had serious conversations with religious leaders who were completely missing the point. Their legalistic approach focused their eyes so much on themselves and their rules that they couldn't see the miraculous gift right in front of them. These religious leaders were overwhelming the people, leading them astray, and certainly not bringing peace. So Jesus spent one of the last sermons of His life telling His disciples how to keep their "eyes on the prize," so to speak. There is an end goal. A finish line. And if we are prepared for it, it will hold eternal peace.

In our world today, we are bombarded with overwhelming messages. Daily life is difficult enough; then add an uncertain world, constant bad news, death and disasters ... It is enough to make anyone feel like things are out of control. And to a degree this feeling is right. Most things are out of our control. However, we can know the One who is in control. And we can know that He has the answers and the end in sight. Therefore, we can know peace, even in this crazy world. Because **peace is keeping our eyes on eternity with Jesus.** When our eyes are fixed on eternity, we can rest in knowing God has a plan. And while we wait for Him to return in victory, we do everything we can to spread His love to this broken, frightened world.

Someday, peace will be our everyday reality, for all of eternity, when Jesus comes back to take us home. In the words of Revelation 22:20, *"Amen. Come, Lord Jesus!"*

WEEK eight

WEEK 8 / DAY 36

Matthew 26:1-35

MAJOR MOMENT
Jesus prepared His disciples for His coming death.

Starting here in Matthew 26 and running through the end of the book, we have the climax of Jesus' story. Here the focus turns to the purpose of Jesus' coming to earth as a man: He came to die. Namely, He came to die for you and me.

- In Matthew 26:2, we learn an important detail. What event or "holiday" was happening at the time of Jesus' death?

It is incredibly significant that Jesus' death aligned with this celebration. Read Exodus 12:21-28. In this Exodus account, the Israelites were about to be freed from slavery! But first "the passover" had to take place.

- What did this first Passover look like or involve?

Matthew 26:3-5 says that the chief priests and elders were plotting to kill Jesus. It also mentions another villain in verse 14: Judas Iscariot.

- How much money did Judas receive to betray Jesus? We will be coming back to this in a few days!

Religious leaders plotting death, a friend betraying Jesus, Jesus trying to prepare His disciples for His journey to the cross ... and sandwiched in the middle of it all is a beautiful example of worship and faithfulness.

- Read Matthew 26:6-13. What words would you use to describe this woman's act of worship? (For example: "generous," etc.)

This woman had no idea she was beautifully preparing Jesus for burial. (v. 12) She didn't perform this act so she could be remembered by all who hear the gospel. (v. 13) Yet these all occurred by God's hand.

- How does it bring you peace to remember that you never know the full scope or eternal significance of your obedience and worship to God?

Before we leave the story of Jesus' anointing at Bethany, let's look at some details in John's account of the same event (John 12:1-8) that will give us even more insight as we continue.

- In John's account of Jesus' anointing, which disciple specifically complained about the cost of the oil?

- Why did he have this complaint? (v. 6)

Judas is such an interesting character to study. On the outside, he appeared to care for the poor. On the inside, he only thought of himself. Notice in Matthew 26:21-25 (the Last Supper) that when Jesus told the disciples one of them would betray Him, none of them looked over at Judas. He was not an obvious betrayer. In fact, he played right along with the disciples, asking, *"Is it I, Rabbi?"* (v. 25a). Jesus' ambiguous answer might have veiled the truth from the other disciples, but Judas knew.

- What does studying Judas' character remind us when we think back to Jesus' words in Matthew 7:15-20?

One final thought to end today ...
- In Matthew 26:30, Jesus and the disciples headed to the Mount of Olives, where Jesus knew He was about to be handed over to His death. Yet before that moment, they did what?

Scholars suggest that this final song would have come from Psalm 115-118. Imagine, for a moment, Jesus knowing He is headed for His death. In His last moments, He sings a song. Read the words of Psalm 116, a song He might have sung.
- How does this psalm take on a new life? How might praise bring peace, even in the darkest moments?

WEEK 8 / DAY 37

Matthew 26:36-75

MAJOR MOMENT

Jesus was betrayed, arrested and taken to a Jewish hearing.

Yesterday we saw how Jesus used some of His last moments to sing.

- What else does Jesus do, as seen in Matthew 26:36?

- What emotions did Jesus experience here? (vv. 37-38)

- Sometimes we need the reminder that it is OK not to be OK. What is going on in your life right now that has you down or troubled? Be specific with what you are feeling exactly.

- As you read through Jesus' time in Gethsemane, what do you learn from Him that you can apply to your own situations?

It would be easy to think Jesus was scared of the pain, humiliation and death coming His way. However, this is not at all a complete picture. Like many martyrs, Jesus bravely faced torture and death. This was something altogether bigger ...

- According to verse 39, Jesus specifically asked, *"My Father, if it be possible, let this _____ pass from me …"*

- According to Jeremiah 25:15-16, what does a cup represent?

- How is it described in Revelation 14:10?

- In other words, what was Jesus about to experience that was truly frightening?

Let's pick back up in Matthew 26:47-56. Judas came to the garden and betrayed Jesus, and an angry mob seized Him …
- And His disciples did what? (v. 56b)

- Jesus carried the weight of ultimate loneliness (even the Father would turn His face away in Matthew 27:46). Yet He did it so that you and I might never have to experience that kind of pain. How does knowing this provide peace when you feel abandoned or alone?

Sometimes we look at events in our world, or even our own personal lives, and feel frustrated. Life appears to be out of control. I'm guessing the disciples felt this way as they watched the night unfold. However, look at Jesus' words.

- Jesus looked at Judas, His betrayer, and said what? (Matthew 26:50a)

- When a disciple pulled a sword, Jesus reminded him God could send thousands of angels if He wanted. Yet what had to be fulfilled? (v. 54)

- When the mob came with swords and clubs, Jesus said they could have seized Him at the temple any time, but they hadn't. Why? (vv. 55-56)

In other words, God was in total control. Even as Jesus was tried by the Jewish high priest and elders, accused by *"many false witnesses"* (v. 60), and labeled a blasphemer who *"deserve[d] death"* (v. 66). The time frame and the unfolding of events were all according to God's plan.

- How does knowing this bring you peace (as Jesus has here) when the world feels chaotic?

WEEK 8 / DAY 38

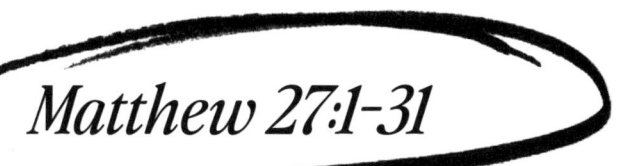
Matthew 27:1-31

MAJOR MOMENT

Jesus faced a Roman hearing and was sentenced to be crucified.

Yesterday we studied how Jesus faced a Jewish hearing and was found guilty of blasphemy. They believed Jesus deserved death for His "crime." However, Rome had put in law that the death penalty was under their jurisdiction. In other words, technically only Rome could punish someone by death. This is why the religious leaders handed Jesus to Pilate, the governor and Roman prefect of Judea.

When Judas fully saw the intentions of the religious leaders, he *"changed his mind ..."* (Matthew 27:3).
- What did Judas do with the money when he changed his mind? (vv. 3-5)

- What did the chief priests do with it? (vv. 6-7)

- Read Zechariah 11:12-13. Realize that Zechariah was written hundreds of years before Jesus was crucified. What does it say?

- Early Church tradition suggests this field the leaders bought with Judas' money was south of Jerusalem in the Hinnom Valley. Read Jeremiah 19:1-3. What similarities do you find here?

In yesterday's reading, after Peter denied Jesus, when he remembered Jesus' words, he *"went out and wept bitterly"* (Matthew 26:75). In today's reading, Judas *"changed his mind"* (Matthew 27:3). The Greek word for this, *metamelomai*, means "to regret."[1]

- What do you think is the difference between repentance and regret?

_____
_____
_____
_____

When Jesus was brought to Pilate, the Jewish leaders were forced to find a political accusation against Jesus to give Him the death penalty. So they accused Him of terrorism, tax evasion and treason. (Luke 23:2) Bogus claims, yet Jesus did nothing to try to defend Himself. This shocked Pilate …

- Yet what did Isaiah 53:7 prophesy?

_____
_____
_____
_____

Pilate wanted to find a way out of this mess, so he turned to an old custom of releasing a prisoner at Passover. Pilate offered the people two choices. He could release Jesus OR Barabbas.

- Read both John 18:40 and Mark 15:7. What do we learn about Barabbas?

_____
_____
_____
_____

Barabbas was *"a notorious prisoner"* (Matthew 27:16). He was a thief, a murderer and a rebel. And yet, in a very foretelling turn of events, Jesus, who was completely innocent, was called upon to die in his place.

- In what ways are we the "Barabbas" in this story? What is your reaction to picturing yourself being set free from crimes you clearly committed? What about seeing Jesus endure the punishment you should have received?

_____
_____
_____
_____

Pilate was convinced Jesus was innocent. Yet Pilate would not let Jesus go free …
- Read John 19:12. The Jewish leaders threatened Pilate by appealing to his loyalty to who?

- Pilate's job was at stake. So instead of doing the right thing, the hard thing, Pilate caved to the crowd. He *"washed his hands"* and said he was *"innocent of this man's blood"* (Matthew 27:24). Yet why was that not really true? And what reminder might that bring to our own lives today?

In the Roman legal code, scourging always preceded capital punishment. They did this so the prisoner would die more quickly on the cross.[2] The person's hands would be tied to a pillar and their back bared to receive lashes from a whip tied with sharp instruments. The lashing would break the skin, often exposing the victim's bones and intestines. Roman soldiers were also notorious for playing cruel games of mockery with their prisoners.
- Read the words of Isaiah 50:6. What was foretold?

As we end today, let's look at Matthew 27:20. It says the religious leaders *"persuaded"* the crowd. This crowd that waved palm branches when Jesus entered on Sunday was crying "Crucify Him!" on Friday. Oh, how easy it is to get swept up with the crowd in only a moment.
- Who has a voice in your ear? How do you determine who to listen to? What can you do today to make sure you don't get swept into something you will later regret?

Matthew 27:32-66

WEEK 8 / DAY 39

MAJOR MOMENT
Jesus died and was buried in a tomb.

Imagine, for a moment, you are a Jew who lives in the far regions of North Africa. You plan a special trip. You are going to celebrate Passover in Jerusalem! You are going to see the temple and gather with your people. What a day! Only, when you arrive, the city is in chaos. Roman soldiers and Jews alike are riled up about some criminal. The streets are packed as you try to move through. And out of nowhere, a Roman soldier grabs you by the arm, pushes you to the street and demands you carry the humiliating cross this criminal is too weak to carry Himself. (Matthew 27:32)

- Describe a time when you have felt like life hit you unexpectedly.

_____
_____
_____
_____
_____
_____

Mark 15:21 describes Simon of Cyrene, the man who carried Jesus' cross, as *"the father of Alexander and Rufus."* This leads us to think, when Mark was written, these two sons must have been well-known members of the Church. Interesting. It makes me wonder what exactly Simon experienced that day. I think it is safe to say Simon came to Jerusalem to sacrifice a lamb and instead found the Lamb of God sacrificed for him.

- How does this look into Simon's life give you peace when your life takes an unexpected turn?

_____
_____
_____
_____
_____
_____

Let's take a few moments now to look at some Old Testament scriptures and line them up with what we read in Matthew 27 today.

- In Matthew 27:34, Jesus was offered wine mixed with gall. Gall was a poisonous herb. In Matthew 27:48, He was offered sour wine. What does Psalm 69:21 say?

- When we studied Psalm 22 last week, we read in verse 18, *"they divide my garments among them, and for my clothing they cast lots."* How was this fulfilled in Matthew 27?

- In Psalm 22:7, it says, *"All who see me mock me; they make mouths at me; they wag their heads."* How was this fulfilled in Matthew 27?

In Matthew 27:50 it says Jesus *"yielded up his spirit."* The Greek word for yielded *(aphiēmi)* means "to send forth" or "to dismiss."[1] In other words, it is by the will and word of the sender.

- How does this align with Jesus' words in John 10:18? And why does this matter?

Jesus was dead. Really and truly dead. This matters. This was not some hoax. And this was not just the death of another man. God wanted that to be very clear, so He gave numerous testimonies for us to read and believe. Matthew recorded many of these so we could have the evidence we need to have faith!

- Read the section called "Testimony to Jesus' Death" on the next page of your study guide. What stands out to you?

- Why is it important that Jesus truly died? (Read Hebrews 9:25-26: It was by the sacrifice of Himself that Jesus put away what? Read Romans 5:10: It is by the death of Jesus that we are what?)

- As we have looked through Matthew's testimonies regarding Jesus' death, why do you think it is important that our faith is backed by evidence?

- What evidence have you seen in your own life that is a testimony to God's power, goodness and redemption?

Testimony to Jesus' Death

MATTHEW 27:45 - DARKNESS
A darkness covered the earth from noon until 3 p.m. Many, many people would be able to attest to whether or not this happened (the same is true for the earthquakes mentioned in verse 51). Also, there are people today who try to dismiss this event as a solar eclipse; however, Passover occurred during a full moon, and a solar eclipse can occur only during a new moon.[1]

MATTHEW 27:51 - CURTAIN OF THE TEMPLE TORN
Not only was this event miraculous, but the symbolism was immense. The curtain separated the people from God's presence. Only the high priest could enter the Most Holy Place, and only once a year, on the Day of Atonement. However, Jesus paid the ultimate atonement and gave us all access to God.

MATTHEW 27:52 - DEAD WERE RAISED
We do not know who these people were exactly, but for those who encountered these once-dead people, the testimony of someone they knew to be dead, and who had been dead for some time, was definitely convincing.

MATTHEW 27:54 - GENTILES BELIEVED
These were soldiers who were accustomed to seeing crucifixions and death. And yet there was something so very different about the death of Jesus that even unbelieving, pagan, hardened Roman guards cried out, *"Truly this was the Son of God!"*

MATTHEW 27:55-56 - WOMEN WITNESSES
Many of the women who followed Jesus, and whose families had become followers of Jesus, witnessed the entire event from a distance. They saw it with their own eyes. They had not scattered, as many of the disciples had, but were present at His death.

MATTHEW 27:57-60 - RICH MAN WITH NOTHING TO GAIN
Joseph of Arimathea was a rich man. He also had power as a member of the Sanhedrin, the Jewish council. (Luke 23:50-51) Joseph risked both power and wealth to ask for Jesus' body. He would have also caused himself to become unclean by coming in contact with a dead body and would not have been able to eat the Passover meal.[2] However, by personally preparing the body, Joseph could attest to the fact that Jesus had truly died.

WEEK 8 / DAY 40

Matthew 28

MAJOR MOMENT
Jesus rose to life!

Yesterday we established that Jesus really and truly died. This is important because if Jesus genuinely died, then His resurrection on the third day is everything. It is the backbone to Christianity and all we believe and look toward. Let's jump into today's reading.

- Read Matthew 28:6a and fill in the blanks to the three parts. Out beside each part, write a summary in your own words. (I've done the first for you.)

    "He is _____ _____,"   (This tomb is EMPTY!)
    "for he _____ _____,"   (_____)
    "as he _____."   (_____)

- Now let's look at the end of verse 6. What did the angel invite the women to do? Why was that important?

After receiving instructions from the angel, the women departed from Jesus' empty tomb *"with fear and great joy"* (v. 8). I appreciate the realness of that statement.

- Do you sometimes feel that following Jesus is both wonderful and scary? Why or why not? What words would you perhaps use to describe what it is like to follow Jesus?

Jesus Christ demonstrated His sacrificial love when He died. And He demonstrated His overwhelming power when He rose again! Together, that combination of love and power, death and resurrection, is what makes Christianity different from any other religion. Jesus proved that He is the Son of God and that eternal life is real.

- Read Romans 8:11. If we believe in Jesus, then we can know that the same power that raised Christ from the dead can do what for us, too?

There is something so ordinary, and yet so extraordinary, in Matthew 28:9 that it just makes me smile.

- What is the first word that Matthew records the resurrected Jesus saying?

- Talk about the biggest and best "hi!" this world has ever heard! Imagine the moment you meet Jesus face to face. Can you hear His "hello"? What does it sound like to you?

When Jesus rose from the grave, He **defeated** Satan. Death and sin have no power under the name of Jesus. But that doesn't mean the enemy took that defeat sitting down.

- Read about the guards and chief priests in Matthew 28:11-15. Then read John 8:44. How do these verses fit together?

Matthew ends his book with Jesus' words to *"Go ... and make disciples of all nations ..."* (Matthew 28:19). We often refer to this as the Great Commission.

- What do you believe it means to *"make disciples"*? Think back to what we have seen between Jesus and His disciples. What might we learn from this example?

_____
_____
_____
_____
_____
_____
_____
_____

Matthew's account of Jesus has taught us so much about how we can have peace in this crazy, chaotic world. And there is perhaps no verse that brings more peace than the last verse of Matthew.

- Copy the last sentence of Matthew 28:20. How does that leave you with peace today?

_____
_____
_____
_____
_____
_____
_____
_____

Throughout our study of Matthew, we have referenced the life of Jesus as a guide toward peace. To live a better way, Jesus' way, we, too, need to *"Come, see the place where he lay"* (Matthew 28:6b). The tomb, my friends, is empty, and that means everything. This weekend, let's arrive at our final stop.

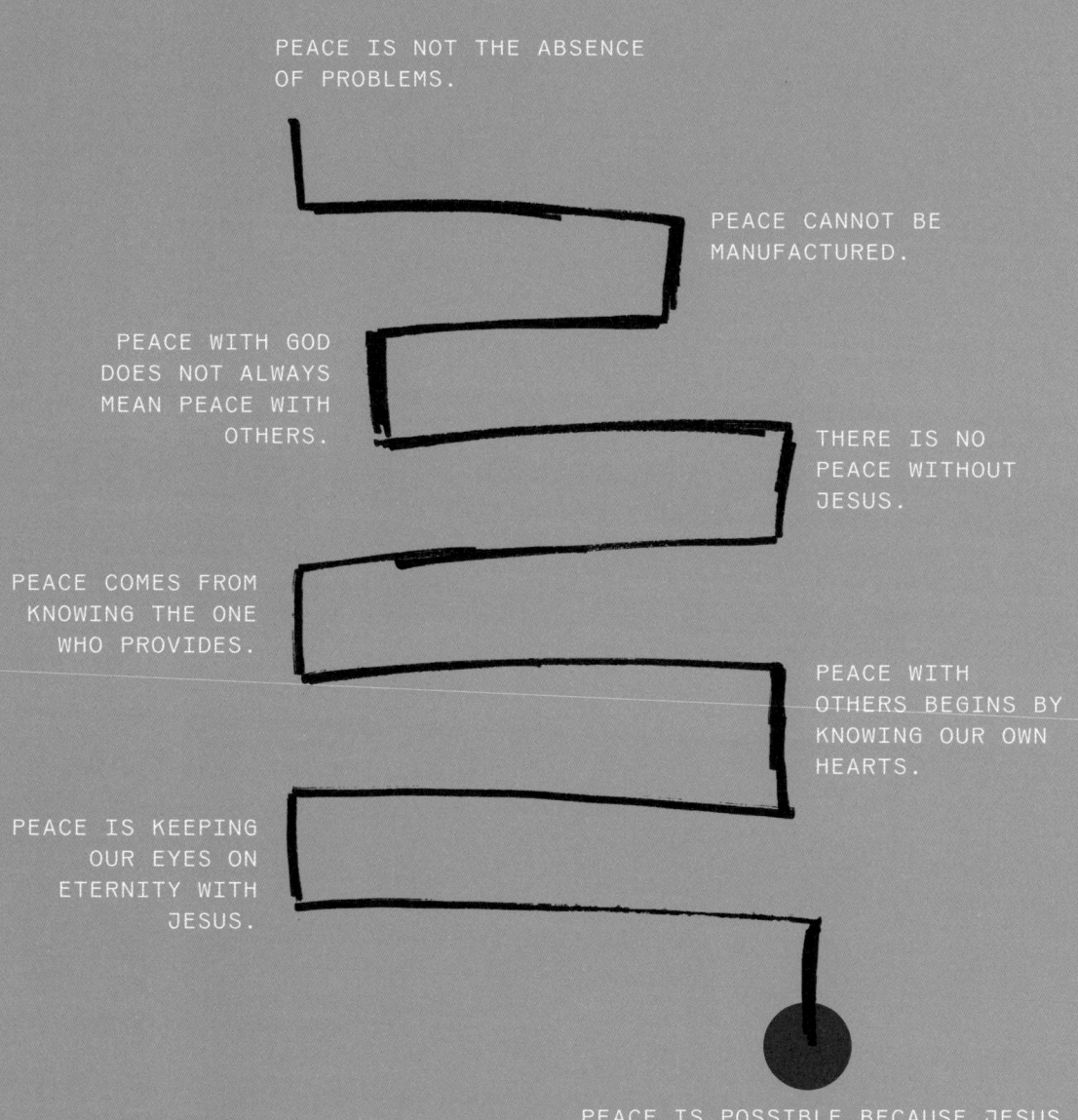

PEACE IS NOT THE ABSENCE OF PROBLEMS.

PEACE CANNOT BE MANUFACTURED.

PEACE WITH GOD DOES NOT ALWAYS MEAN PEACE WITH OTHERS.

THERE IS NO PEACE WITHOUT JESUS.

PEACE COMES FROM KNOWING THE ONE WHO PROVIDES.

PEACE WITH OTHERS BEGINS BY KNOWING OUR OWN HEARTS.

PEACE IS KEEPING OUR EYES ON ETERNITY WITH JESUS.

PEACE IS POSSIBLE BECAUSE JESUS IS ALIVE.

Weekend Reflection

Peace is possible because Jesus is alive.

In our reading this week, we witnessed Jesus go through excruciating anxiety, abandonment, pain, ridicule and death. Jesus understands what it is like to live in a harsh and hurting world. He recognizes there are times when peace feels elusive. So Jesus did what only Jesus could do: He faced the problem head-on. He took on the sin that has messed up our hearts, and He stared down the death that threatens our bodies; He brought them to a tomb and declared that only one would be coming out alive!

And friends, when the world looked to be at its darkest, most hopeless moment, Sunday morning came, and the stone was rolled away, and Jesus Christ, our Friend, our Lord, our Savior, walked out of that tomb. Which means no matter how the world looks at this very moment, we can know without a doubt that if we have Jesus *we will be OK*. Death cannot touch our souls, and sin cannot keep us from eternity. Jesus made sure of it. **Peace is possible because Jesus is alive.**

And because Jesus is alive, His words in Matthew 28:20 echo true for all of us. He is with us. Always. To the end of the age. That is peace for today and tomorrow and eternity.

IN CASE YOU WERE *Wondering*

"'Behold, the virgin shall conceive and bear a son, and they shall call his name Immanuel' (which means, God with us)." (Matthew 1:23)

Here in this verse, Matthew quotes an Old Testament prophecy: Isaiah 7:14. This prophetic moment points not only to the fact that Jesus is the fulfillment of Old Testament prophecy, connecting the Old and New Testaments as one gospel, but also to the unveiling of Jesus' divinity and purpose. The fact that His conception was not ordinary but miraculous (*"the virgin shall conceive and bear a son"*) confirms His divinity.

Along with the revelation of Jesus' divinity in His virgin birth, we see the Hebrew translation of "Immanuel," one of Jesus' names, literally means "God with us"! In this explanation of Jesus' name, Matthew draws a direct correlation between God and His Son, claiming that God, through His Son, came to be with His people. Not only was Jesus' birth beyond ordinary, but His nature is divine, and His purpose is clear. God Himself came to be with us and is still with us!

-NORA TATINA

"Therefore do not be anxious about tomorrow, for tomorrow will be anxious for itself. Sufficient for the day is its own trouble." (Matthew 6:34)

When I think of being anxious or troubled, I think of things falling apart, of things being broken and fractured. The phrase "falling to pieces" perhaps grasps the concept well. To be anxious and worried is not an easy space to live in. In fact, though many things about following Jesus are not easy, Jesus said anxious living is not the way to live in His Kingdom. Not being anxious means refraining from negatively thinking our tomorrow is falling apart — and we do this by seeking the Kingdom where our Prince of Peace rules. The Greek word for peace, *eirēnē*, means things coming together, being whole, being one. Jesus is drawing us away from fracture and brokenness in our inner world to discover wholeness and oneness in Him with the Father and Holy Spirit. If God, who is perfectly one within Himself, brings wholeness to creation, we can rest assured that His plan for us is no different.

-JILL BOYD

"Ask, and it will be given to you; seek, and you will find; knock, and it will be opened to you." (Matthew 7:7)

These words of Jesus are a lesson on prayer. It is interesting to note that the three verbs, *ask, seek* and *knock,* are in the present progressive tense in Greek; therefore, the sentence could read, *"keep asking ... keep seeking ... keep knocking."* Pursuing God in prayer is never futile. There is always an answer in the asking, a finding in the seeking, and an opening in the knocking.

Jesus followed up His command with an analogy about parents and children. (Matthew 7:8-10) Parents desire good things for their children, and even though parents might not give exactly what their child asks for, they will give what will benefit the child most. We must remember God's kindness as our heavenly Father. With each step of prayer, asking, seeking, knocking, we come to the throne of the King ... and the King is our Father. God will be gracious to hear us and give us exactly what we need, according to His wisdom and love, as we seek His will.

-BRONWYN CARDWELL

"Whoever finds his life will lose it, and whoever loses his life for my sake will find it." (Matthew 10:39)

Matthew 10:39 defines being a *disciple* of Christ. The gift of salvation comes when we believe, and it's free. But discipleship — truly following Jesus — comes with a cost. The self-centeredness of humanity has always been a problem, and here Jesus addresses that issue. To follow Jesus, we must stop holding our lives in our own hands; we must die to old, sinful habits; old, unhelpful traditions; and old, wrong beliefs. Sometimes the cost is separation from family and friends and from worldly things we love. Not everyone will make this choice to pursue the sacrificial life of a disciple. However, as we also see in passages like Mark 10:29-30 and Luke 9:61-62, true believers in Christ are also disciples of Christ, and they are on a new path to a life held in the hands of the great Creator. The life we "find" will be well worth the cost.

-CHERYL DALE

"Come to me, all who labor and are heavy laden, and I will give you rest. Take my yoke upon you, and learn from me, for I am gentle and lowly in heart, and you will find rest for your souls. For my yoke is easy, and my burden is light." (Matthew 11:28-30)

In our modern-day culture, the agricultural concept of a yoke might seem a little foreign. Maybe you've seen pictures in a history book of two oxen joined together by a large wooden frame as they pulled heavy farm equipment through a field. The image that comes to mind might seem harsh and heavy and restrictive, and that is true — it can be. We read many examples in the Bible of how God's people were burdened by a yoke of slavery (Leviticus 26:13) and a yoke of oppression. (Isaiah 14:25;

Jeremiah 2:20; Ezekiel 34:27)

But in these three verses of Matthew, Jesus offers a different kind of yoke. Rather than being forced to carry a heavy load by being connected to the wrong things or by trying to do everything on our own, we can connect ourselves to God. We don't have to bear the heavy weight of our own sins any longer. As we follow Christ and study His Word, we become His disciples. By learning how to follow God's ways and trust in His sovereignty, we find true rest.

-SANDY JOHNSON

"But Jesus looked at them and said, 'With man this is impossible, but with God all things are possible.'" (Matthew 19:26)

The context surrounding this verse is about salvation, which is only made possible through God. This statement comes after a rich man questioned Jesus about how to earn eternal life. (Matthew 19:16-22) The man assumed his good works would suffice, but Jesus raised the bar to include the man's heart. When instructed to sell his possessions and give to the poor, the man walked away sorrowful because his attachment to his possessions made him incapable of obeying and following Jesus.

Wealth was considered to be a sign of God's blessing, so the disciples were astonished the rich man's treasures and good works were not enough to save him. Jesus used this as a teaching moment to clarify that it's impossible for someone to be saved by their own merit, strength or status. Only by declaring our absolute need for Him, letting go of our will and choosing to follow Him, do we demonstrate faith in God to do the impossible through us.

-JEN ALLEE

"And he took a cup, and when he had given thanks he gave it to them, saying, 'Drink of it, all of you, for this is my blood of the covenant, which is poured out for many for the forgiveness of sins.'" (Matthew 26:27-28)

In the final, precious moments of His life, Jesus gifted His disciples with the knowledge of what the new blood covenant would look like. For Christians, Jesus has completely transformed the Jewish Passover meal to what is now called the Lord's Supper. I am sure this astonished the disciples with more to process about the Messiah.

The heart of our Lord has always been to set His people free from sin. In order for us to be set free, there first had to be a covenant involving the sacrifice of animals, but in this passage of Scripture, Jesus prophesied about the moment where His own blood would be poured out as a drink offering for the forgiveness of sins. Jesus took the cup of wine and said, *"Drink of it, all of you, for this is **my** blood* of the covenant, *which is poured out for many for the forgiveness of sins"* (vv. 27-28, emphasis added). Through the reinterpretation of the wine as His blood, Jesus drew attention to God's deliverance of His people in Exodus and how this pointed to His upcoming suffering on the cross for our sins. His blood was spilled for the forgiveness of sin. (Hebrews 9:22)

-CHRISTY MOORE

"Go therefore and make disciples of all nations, baptizing them in the name of the Father and of the Son and of the Holy Spirit ..." (Matthew 28:19)

Though often used to encourage overseas missions, the actual command of "The Great Commission," as it is dubbed, is for all believers to *"make disciples"* whether we stay at home or go abroad. This command is flanked by three descriptions of how we make disciples:

- *"Go"* tells us we make disciples as we go throughout life. (Deuteronomy 6:7)
- *"Baptizing"* tells us, among other things, that we make disciples by preaching the gospel to unbelievers so they repent, join the family of God, and identify with His death and resurrection.
- *"Teaching"* tells us we make disciples by instructing believers to live out their commitment through obedience to Jesus' instruction (Matthew 28:20).

Jesus, the King with all authority, (Matthew 28:18) gives this command to His people. In this way, we become the answers to our own prayers for laborers for the harvest, (Matthew 9:37-38) multiplying disciples for His Kingdom.

-VERA CHRISTIAN

"But the angel said to the women, 'Do not be afraid, for I know that you seek Jesus who was crucified. He is not here, for he has risen, as he said. Come, see the place where he lay.'" (Matthew 28:5-6)

What a proclamation of power and truth about Christ's resurrection, concluding with an invitation to the women to come and see Jesus' vacant grave. As the angel announcements in Scripture always go, the emphasis was on Jesus. As the women listened, they were reminded of the words Jesus had spoken, and it was confirmed to them that Jesus did exactly as He proclaimed He would do.

This declaration brought hope and assurance to these women who came seeking Jesus. That same hope and assurance can be ours today. Resurrection is the essence of the gospel of Jesus Christ. An empty tomb and the resurrected Christ, triumphing over death, opened the way for the birth of the Church and a new era. This resurrection separates Christianity from every other religion. We have a risen Savior whom we can trust, and who desires and deserves our belief in Him. The tomb is still empty!

-SHARON BOLLINGER

End Notes

WELCOME TO MATTHEW
[1] Wiersbe, Warren W. *Be Loyal: Following the King of Kings.* NT Commentary: Matthew. Colorado Springs, CO: David C Cook, 1980. pp 19.

WHY IS THIS WORLD SO CHAOTIC?
[1] Smith, Gregory A. "About Three-in-Ten U.S. Adults Are Now Religiously Unaffiliated." *Pew Research Center.* https://www.pewforum.org/2021/12/14/about-three-in-ten-u-s-adults-are-now-religiously-unaffiliated/. Accessed February 2022.

ALL ABOUT THE AUTHOR
[1] Alexander Whyte of Edinburgh, as cited in: Wiersbe, Warren W. *Be Loyal: Following the King of Kings.* NT Commentary: Matthew. Colorado Springs, CO: David C Cook, 1980. pp 22-23.

DAY 5
[1] Platt, David. *Exalting Jesus in Matthew.* Christ-Centered Exposition, edited by David Platt, Daniel L. Akin, and Tony Merida. Nashville, TN: Holman, 2013. pp. 69.

[2] Platt, David. *Exalting Jesus in Matthew.* Christ-Centered Exposition, edited by David Platt, Daniel L. Akin, and Tony Merida. Nashville, TN: Holman, 2013. pp. 71.

[3] Platt, David. *Exalting Jesus in Matthew.* Christ-Centered Exposition, edited by David Platt, Daniel L. Akin, and Tony Merida. Nashville, TN: Holman, 2013. pp. 72.

[4] Moore, Russell. *Tempted and Tried: Temptation and the Triumph of Christ.* Wheaton: Crossway, 2011. pp. 131.

DAY 6
[1] Wiersbe, Warren W. *Be Loyal: Following the King of Kings.* NT Commentary: Matthew. Colorado Springs, CO: David C Cook, 1980. pp 46.

DAY 7
[1] *The ESV Study Bible.* Wheaton, Ill: Crossway, 2008. pp. 1830.

DAY 8
[1] Wiersbe, Warren W. *Be Loyal: Following the King of Kings.* NT Commentary: Matthew. Colorado Springs, CO: David C Cook, 1980. pp 59.

DAY 9
[1] Simpson, Jon. "Finding Brand Success in The Digital World." *Forbes Agency Council.* https://www.forbes.com/sites/forbesagencycouncil/2017/08/25/finding-brand-success-in-the-digital-world/?sh=80c67a0626e2. Accessed February 2022.

[2] "Average child gets $6,500 worth of toys in their lifetime." *SWNS Media Group.* https://swnsdigital.com/us/2016/11/average-child-gets-6500-worth-of-toys-in-their-lifetime/. Accessed February 2022.

[3] Wiersbe, Warren W. *Be Loyal: Following the King of Kings.* NT Commentary: Matthew. Colorado Springs, CO: David C Cook, 1980. pp 60.

DAY 11
[1] Kidner, D. *Psalms 1–72: an introduction and commentary* (Vol. 15.). Downers Grove, IL: InterVarsity Press, 1973. pp. 168.

DAY 12
[1] Platt, David. *Exalting Jesus in Matthew.* Christ-Centered Exposition, edited by David Platt, Daniel L. Akin, and Tony Merida. Nashville, TN: Holman, 2013. pp. 104-115.

[2] *The Unexpected King: Matthew's Account of Jesus.* Bible Study Fellowship. 1963-2021. pp. 97.

DAY 13
[1] Platt, David. *Exalting Jesus in Matthew.* Christ-Centered Exposition, edited by David Platt, Daniel L. Akin, and Tony Merida. Nashville, TN: Holman, 2013. pp. 119.

DAY 15
[1] Platt, David. *Exalting Jesus in Matthew.* Christ-Centered Exposition, edited by David Platt, Daniel L. Akin, and Tony Merida. Nashville, TN: Holman, 2013. pp. 145-146.

[2] McGrath, Alister. "When Doubt Becomes Unbelief." *Tabletalk* 16, No. 1 (January 1992): pp. 8-10.

DAY 16
[1] Storms, Sam. "Legalism: 5 Questions to Ask Yourself." *Crossway*. https://www.crossway.org/articles/legalism-5-questions-to-ask-yourself/. Accessed April 2022.

[2] Carson, D. A. *Matthew*. In F. E. Gaebelein (Ed.), The Expositor's Bible Commentary: Matthew, Mark, Luke (Vol 8). Grand Rapids, MI: Zondervan Publishing House, 1984. pp. 290-292.

DAY 19
[1] *The Unexpected King: Matthew's Account of Jesus*. Bible Study Fellowship. 1963-2021. pp. 138.

DAY 22
[1] *"splanchnizomai."* Thompson, Jeremy. Bible Sense Lexicon: Dataset Documentation. Bellingham, WA: Faithlife, 2015.

DAY 24
[1] *"deny."* Merriam-Webster, I. *Merriam-Webster's collegiate dictionary*. (Eleventh ed.). Springfield, MA: Merriam-Webster, Inc., 2003.

DAY 25
[1] Barton, B., Comfort, P., Osborne, G., Taylor, L.K., Veerman, D. *Life Application New Testament Commentary*. Wheaton, IL: Tyndale House Publishers, Inc., 2001. pp. 78.

DAY 26
[1] *The ESV Study Bible*. Wheaton, Ill: Crossway, 2008. pp. 1859.

[2] ibid.

DAY 27
[1] *The ESV Study Bible*. Wheaton, Ill: Crossway, 2008. pp. 1860.

[2] *The Unexpected King: Matthew's Account of Jesus*. Bible Study Fellowship. 1963-2021. pp. 207

DAY 31
[1] *The ESV Study Bible*. Wheaton, Ill: Crossway, 2008. pp. 1124.

DAY 32
[1] Wiersbe, Warren W. *Be Loyal: Following the King of Kings*. NT Commentary: Matthew. Colorado Springs, CO: David C Cook, 1980. pp 202.

DAY 34
[1] Barton, B., Comfort, P., Osborne, G., Taylor, L.K., Veerman, D. *Life Application New Testament Commentary*. Wheaton, IL: Tyndale House Publishers, Inc., 2001. pp. 107.

DAY 38
[1] *"metamelomai."* Swanson, J. (1997). *Dictionary of Biblical Languages with Semantic Domains: Greek (New Testament)* (electronic ed.). Oak Harbor: Logos Research Systems, Inc.

[2] Barton, B., Comfort, P., Osborne, G., Taylor, L.K., Veerman, D. *Life Application New Testament Commentary*. Wheaton, IL: Tyndale House Publishers, Inc., 2001. pp. 121.

DAY 39
[1] *"aphiēmi."* Swanson, J. (1997). *Dictionary of Biblical Languages with Semantic Domains: Greek (New Testament)* (electronic ed.). Oak Harbor: Logos Research Systems, Inc.

Testimony to Jesus' Death
[1] *The ESV Study Bible*. Wheaton, Ill: Crossway, 2008. pp. 1886.

[2] Wiersbe, Warren W. *Be Loyal: Following the King of Kings*. NT Commentary: Matthew. Colorado Springs, CO: David C Cook, 1980. pp 261.

Notes:

Notes:

Notes:

Notes:

Notes:

KEEP THE MOMENTUM OF
TIME IN GOD'S WORD GOING.

Join us for:

MAKE IT COUNT

*Move Past Your Past
and Live With Purpose Today*

A DEUTERONOMY STUDY GUIDE

AVAILABLE NOVEMBER 2022 AT P31BOOKSTORE.COM